SECRETS OF SUFFERING

SECRETS OF SUFFERING

The biblical formula to understanding suffering

Dr. T.A. Nalian

ELM HILL

A Division of
HarperCollins Christian Publishing

www.elmhillbooks.com

Secrets of Suffering
The biblical formula to understanding suffering

Published in Nashville, Tennessee, by Elm Hill, an imprint of Thomas Nelson. Elm Hill and Thomas Nelson are registered trademarks of HarperCollins Christian Publishing, Inc.

Elm Hill titles may be purchased in bulk for educational, business, fund-raising, or sales promotional use. For information, please e-mail SpecialMarkets@ ThomasNelson.com.

All Scripture quotations are from the King James Version. Public domain.

Library of Congress Cataloging-in-Publication Data

Library of Congress Control Number: 2019914942

ISBN 978-1-400329335 (Paperback)
ISBN 978-1-400329342 (Hardbound)
ISBN 978-1-400329359 (eBook)

DEDICATIONS

To Dr. Harry E. Carr, the greatest expositor I have ever known. He was my professor and the one who influenced and instilled in me as a young student of the Bible, whether in preaching or in writing, to "always make plain and simple the wonderful truths of the Bible."

To my beautiful, longsuffering wife, Cheryl, and my precious children, Autumn, Lindsay, Joshua, Elijah and Ezekiel who are the closest and dearest to my heart — Thank you for going on this journey with me.

To the countless of sufferers around the world, who persevere in faith and love for their Lord; awaiting patiently the end of their faith, conformity into the image of Jesus Christ God's son!

TABLE OF CONTENTS

FORWARD

My name is Dr. Tom Williams, Pastor of Liberty Baptist Church in Massillon, Ohio. I have been in ministry for over 35 years, and I'm a veteran of the Vietnam War. I first met Terry while booking a Stand Strength Team crusade at our church. Terry and I connected during our first phone call, I could hear in his voice a burden and compassion for the kids and teens in this country. Terry truly has a burning desire to help everyone of every age and is constantly on his phone helping someone who is suffering in some way.

After reading this book, I can honestly say that it is the very best book that I have ever read besides the Bible. There are so many people that are suffering today and this book is in God's time. It is a very complex world, but this book will give you a simple way to get you through the suffering because it is God's way. Secrets of Suffering is a must-read for everyone and there is no question that our Lord guided Terry's hand in writing this book. I am not trying to over glorify the book or Terry because I give all the glory to our Lord Jesus Christ. I personally have suffered many things in my life: being critically wounded in Vietnam; cancer in my family, including me; severe family problems; and many other things. The Secrets of Suffering was a blessing to me and I looked at suffering in a different way than I ever had before.

It is a great honor to write the forward of such a great book, just being a part of this book that will change many lives. I am pleading with you right now as if I am standing right next to you. Find a quiet place, take your time, take down notes and let the Lord speak to you through this book because He is all through this book. Secrets of Suffering will change your thoughts of suffering, which will change your attitude, which will change your walk in the Lord. You will be helped and will be able to help others after reading this book. Terry has suffered many things in his life, so he is writing from experience which means the writing of this book came from his heart.

I pray that you take this book seriously and with an open heart and ask that the Lord teach you on The Secrets of Suffering. Knowing that you have suffered or you are suffering now or you will suffer in this journey called life, so please read this book and get the help you truly need.

Dr. Tom Williams
Pastor of Liberty Baptist Church
Massillon, Ohio

PREFACE

"Here we go again," you say, "another book on suffering." I know many heavyweights such as James Dobson, Zig Ziggler, Philip Yancy, Chuck Swindoll, J. Vernon McGee, John Hagee, C.S. Lewis, and many others have written and spoken prolifically on the subject. By no means am I putting myself in a league with these men, but I am compelled to write to you on this subject. I am not writing from the position of conjecture, speculation, hypothesis or assumption, but from the platform of experiential reality. I must be careful here because experience does not dictate doctrine, but pure and right doctrine confirms our experience. Having gone through four personal tragedies in my life does not make me an authority on the subject, but I do have something to say.

The objective of this book is to form in you a persevering faith. A faith that will cause you, through great resolve, to pursue and embrace God, who will bring to pass for you a wonderful eternal consolation, which was born out of all of your suffering. The words that you will subsequently read have been tested, tried, and proven all over the country over the last 28 years. During this time, I have delivered many sermons, lectures, teachings, radio messages, and Q & A television programs on the subject. The time is far spent. I have now gathered all the data, fragments, parts, and pieces from my own personal journey, coupled with absolute biblical truth. And now dear reader, I want to deliver these wonderful truths to you.

CHAPTER 1

THE ORIGIN OF SUFFERING

*All the mysteries of sin, tragedy, and human suffering will find their fulfill-
ment and finality in the holiness of God as it relates to the free will of man.*

In **Genesis 2:16-17**, God told Adam, *"...Of every tree of the garden
thou mayest freely eat: But of the tree of the knowledge of good and
evil, thou shalt not eat of it: for in the day that thou eatest thereof thou
shalt surely die."* God, in the creation of the material universe, established
many laws. These laws are inescapable. They are the dictum, mandate, and
command of God, by which He has chosen in His sovereignty to govern
the universe. The laws of God were meant for our protection. His laws are a
manifestation of His holy character. By the keeping of, yielding thereto, and
embracing of His laws, we maintain a right and wholesome fellowship with
God. When the laws of God are broken, pure anarchy, sorrows, troubles
and woes will be the result.

Though Adam was in a completely holy and righteous environment, his
righteousness was based on the continuation and determination of his obedience. Before Adam and Eve rebelled against the command of God and
willingly sinned (breaking God's law) no mosquito had ever bitten, and their
bodies had never experienced the decay of growing old. Pain was a completely foreign and unknown concept. Then — BLAM!!! The unthinkable

1

happened. The shock was felt by the entire human race. The whole world - every living thing on land and in the sea - was plunged into depravity, a state of chaos, and sin because of the disobedience of Adam. *"For we know that the whole creation groaneth and travaileth in pain together until now."* **(Romans 8:22)** If Fox News Network, CNN and the Associated Press had been present, the headlines would have read, **"The World Is Under Attack!"**

The source and cause of this known phenomenon is a direct result of the broken law of God. Now, every vile and horrid occurrence has opportunity to flourish and even dominate as a consequence of the futile action of allowing this enemy to pierce the veil of God's holiness and righteousness. The world and its population are exposed to suffering, not because of God, but because of the corruption of man; not because of the fault of God, but because of the foolishness of man. God is not to be blamed – ever. He is the One we must look to for blessing and help through the storm. The foundation, cornerstone, pillar and cause of sorrow and suffering are not of God, but are of man. This must be paramount in our thinking as we continue to deal with this subject matter. We must often remember this reference point as we work through the conflicts and mysteries of suffering.

The law in **Genesis 2:16-17** is God's law of sin and death. He tells us in **Ezekiel 18:4, 20,** *"...The soul that sinneth, it shall die..."* **Romans 3:23a** further declares, *"For the wages of sin is death..."* Before the "fall of man," the world was perfect. Prior to the entrance and introduction of sin into the human race, death, disease, tragedy, war, human cruelty, famine, the aggression of the animal kingdom, violent storms and any other bad thing did not exist. It is safe to say at this point that the cause and origin of all suffering is *sin.*

It is important to understand, though, that not everyone suffering is going through it because of their *own* personal sin and failure. The very simplistic answer is that all are exposed to suffering because we live in a sin-cursed world. Pollution caused by a very small portion of the industrialized world will still impact all who are exposed to it. You may be consumed by trying to find the *reasons* for suffering. God's Word does not focus on the revelation of why we suffer. His Word is more concerned about how we deal with and respond to our suffering. Dwelling on the cause of suffering induces defeat. We are to seek and discipline ourselves to have the right attitude as we endure suffering. This results in victory. The great truth is this: If we cannot change the situation, we must change our attitude.

One day, the holiness of the Lord will fill the entire earth. At that time, the world will be restored to its pre-Adamic state of perfection. In the process of time, we must view all suffering (no matter the source or the cause) as a conduit to help us conform into the image of Jesus Christ, God's Son **(Romans 8:28-30)**.

As a result of the entrance of sin, death is the greatest foe to the human race.

Death and all that comes before it, must acquiesce and surrender its power in utter defeat! Our future is established in victory; we will be triumphant.

A QUESTION TO DEATH

O Death, let me ask you a question. Why are you so cruel and cold?
You move without mercy, taking young and old.
Cries temper not your cold blast.
Brokenness will not suffice you at the last. Your scope is so vast
beyond what any eye can see.
Now talk to me death and answer me.
I am a pallbearer that ushers your loved one into a better place,
filled with God's love, joy, peace, comfort, glory and grace.
Escorted by the Good Shepherd to the street of gold,
the King's Palace, twelve foundations garnished with all manner of
precious stone.
To a land of heavenly rest, green pastures and a sweet song that
fills the air,
Your loved one no longer to know tears, sorrow, pain, or care.
If given a choice, they would no longer desire to be where you are.

For they now behold the brilliance of the bright and Morning Star.

Into His countenance they shall eternally gaze,

forever united with loved ones to sing, worship, and praise.

I too, am subject to HIS will divine.

Do you not now know, understand and see,

I, Death, have been swallowed up in Victory.

CHAPTER 2

THE "WHY?" OF SUFFERING

The sowing process of our life, we control. The reaping process of our life, God controls. He is the Lord of the harvest.

Remember in our former chapter we learned that God is not the cause of our suffering, but He is the cure. God is not the one at fault, but He is the faithful One who will stand with us in all of our sufferings **(2 Timothy 4:17)**. God is not to be blamed, but He is the One who will bless and secure us in every storm **(Mark 4:39)**. The predominance of suffering in the world is due to man breaking the universal laws of God. These laws operate under the premise of "cause and effect," and will take their natural course.

Let me explain. For example, the habitual drug user is not exempt from his or her own body breaking down as a result of the awful addiction. My closest childhood friend, Michael, began using drugs in middle school. He never made it out of high school because he dropped out. His use of drugs robbed him of that goal. It wasn't long before he repeatedly was in trouble with the law and even experienced incarceration as a result of his extensive drug use. Through the process of time, Michael's body began to break down. He experienced many physical complications.

Mike and I played together almost every day when we were kids. We would go hiking in the woods, ride our bikes together. We'd go down to the Rouge River near our home and look for turtles. We'd go tobogganing together. We would stay the night at each other's house. Mike and I had lots of fun together.

But when we were in middle school, Mike's life took another direction. He started hanging out with the drug crowd and asked me to go with him. I'll never forget that time in my life, that turning point. I made a distinct choice. "Michael," I said, "I love you. You are my best friend, but I cannot follow you down this path." I remember saying to him, "Michael, if you don't stop, one day I'm going to get a call and someone is going to tell me that Michael is dead." When I was in my twenties, and pastoring my first church, I received that call. It was Michael's sister, Patty. She said, "Terry," in a melancholy tone, "Michael is dead. We found him on his bed on his back with his eyes rolled up into the back of his head." Michael was about 28 years old when he died. He could never hold down a job. He never got a driver's license and he always lived with his parents. The cause, for Michael, was his choice to use drugs. The effect, and his ultimate outcome, was his death.

I grew up in a corrupted home. I experienced frequent beatings and abuse at the hands of my alcoholic father. My common experience was being hung upside down by the ankles and having my head pounded on the floor, or being dragged by the back of my hair up two flights of stairs and then kicked down from the top. I recall being pinned underneath my dad's heavy body, my face being baptized with his putrid alcoholic breath and spit, while he would scream into my ears. This caused pain to shoot through my entire body. Moreover, I have memories of being held firm by my ankle - and with an open-handed, punishing, palm strike - having the bottoms of my feet struck with repeated blows. All I could do was wriggle, writhe, oscillate, squirm, quiver, and shake in unbearable pain, begging for mercy for the torment to cease. I can recall many backhanded blows and kicks; at times my father would ram my head into a wall.

This is one of four personal tragedies that I will share with you in this book. I grew up a broken kid and turned into a broken adult. After many years of contemplation, and questioning my Savior over these experiences of my youth, I came to understand through His infallible wisdom and His loving guidance, that my earthly father chose a course for himself, but my Heavenly Father ordained me to His eternal purpose, His eternal plan and His specific place for my life **(Jeremiah 1:5; Galatians 1:15; 2 Timothy 1:9)**. As a result of my father's alcohol use and abuse, he suffered many hurts and sorrows. Not only was he in and out of mental institutions and jail, he also needed to make frequent emergency room visits because of automobile accidents, bar fights, and attempted suicides.

When I was 18 years old, resting down in my basement room after coming home from Bible college my freshman year, I recall being shockingly awoken from the blast of a gunshot. I immediately knew what had happened. Dad shot himself! I rushed up the stairs with my hands pushing and thrusting myself against both walls of the staircase to generate more speed, as I climbed from the basement to the first floor of our home. I ran through the kitchen and made a sharp right turn, running through the living room and then through a short hall, which led to my dad's bedroom. Upon entering his room on the left, I saw the .22 caliber rifle slipping out of his hands, exposing the dark blackened gunshot wound in his chest with the smoke of the blast still emanating from the barrel and ascending slowly into the air. His eyes rolled to the back of his head with every facial feature drooping, and his body fell lifeless onto the bed. It was at that moment that I understood all of the horrible effects caused by his choices.

Our family was always in chaos and turmoil. I never knew a day, my entire life, when I could remember a joyful look upon my mother's countenance. Instead she manifested a continual sadness.

As I rode to the hospital in the ambulance, I remember pressing my face against the window with uncontrollable tears, silently begging God to save my dad. It seemed that every image and memory flashed through my mind, with distinct clarity, of all of the offenses and actions that my father had wrought toward me and our family while under the influence of the brew from the abyss of the Underworld. Frame by frame, I saw the multitudes of my beatings and abuse. I saw smashed cars that my father had wrecked while in his drunken stupor, as they would be towed and dropped off at the front of our house. I saw the image of a gun broken over a man's head, and blood all over the sidewalk, because my dad was beating that man to death. I heard all of the screams of my mother and siblings, as the house would frequently erupt as the result of my father's out-of-control rampages while being under the influence. Our home was an insane asylum! At that very moment, I experienced the grace of God, in action in my soul. I was overcome by love not anger, mercy not wrath, comfort and not turmoil toward my dad. God was merciful to me. He heard and answered my prayers; my father survived his attempted suicide.

While growing up, I never saw family structure or my father give my mother any affection. I was never taught anything about personal hygiene or even how to dress myself. I was never given any guidance about anything in life that really mattered. I was left alone in a world of chaos, suffering silently because of one man's choice. The cause: early in Albert Nalian, Sr.'s life, he was influenced by a friend to drink alcohol. The effect: a slow gradual decline of health from dementia. The ultimate result was death.

As a result of drugs and alcohol, children and families all over the world suffer greatly from broken homes and domestic violence. Because of wicked, cruel, and brutal dictatorships, along with false religions and the greed of man, millions of people around the world have been left in the wake of starvation, disease, famine, war and unutterable human suffering. Crimes committed against the human race, along with the masses addicted to pornography and gambling, have plunged untold multitudes into the arena of sorrow and suffering. These things were not God induced but man induced.

CHAPTER 3

The secret of suffering is found in

THE PROMISE

"Every promise of God will come to fruition, but in our perils, with patience and long suffering, we must wait for it."

"Many are the afflictions of the righteous: but the LORD delivereth him out of them all."

(PSALMS 34:19)

The mystery of suffering will be solved when we finally and ultimately stand in the presence of the One who suffered the most. When that time comes, the Revelator of all things will make clear the purpose for our suffering, which is now shrouded in the thick clouds of despair and grief. As the apostle Paul said, we will also be able to say, *"For now we see through a glass, darkly; but then face to face: now I know in part; but then shall I know even as also I am known."* (1 Corinthians 13:12) The moment we make our entrance into heaven, our minds will be fixed on the quaint thought that in the former life we could have had more opportunity for blessing and more opportunity to experience the presence of Christ through suffering. In this chapter, we will see the many forms and faces of what deliverance from our suffering looks like.

9

"I will bless the LORD at all times: his praise shall continually be in my mouth." **(Psalms 34:1)** The resolve of David in this first verse is remarkable. *"I will bless the LORD at all times..."* David is not just referring to the good times, when all is going well and he is at ease. The expression, *"I will"*, shows the determination, stamina, and perseverance of the sweet psalmist of Israel. When the sun is shining and the weather is clement, when the breeze is mild and comforting, and the flowers are blooming and the birds are singing, and when the waters are still, the psalmist blessed the Lord. But when the sun is swallowed up by the dark, stormy clouds of trial and despair, and the flowers are frozen by the winter's pitiless blast, and the birds' melodies can no longer be heard because their voices have been replaced with the cries of an agonized soul, and the waters are now in a tumultuous rage, tossing the vessel of life to and fro with calamitous fervor, the resolve and determination of the psalmist is still the same, *"I will bless the LORD at all times!"*

David, in this psalm, is declaring that when it comes to the matters of suffering, God will always deliver us. In verse four he states, *"I sought the LORD and he heard me, and delivered me from all my fears."* How many of his fears? *All.* Notice verse six, *"This poor man cried, and the LORD heard him, and saved him out of all his troubles."* How many of his troubles? *All.* Now look at verse 17, *"The righteous cry, and the LORD heareth, and delivereth them out of all their troubles."* Let's review. The psalmist had confidence that the Lord would deliver him from: all fears in verse four, all troubles in verse six, and all troubles in verse 17.

Our text **(Psalms 34:19)** has a unique structure. The truth that makes this verse unique is not so much what is obvious, but rather something that is not mentioned at all. Consider: the psalmist is silent concerning the realm, matter, element and sphere of time. While we see and hear the statement of the obvious, "Many are the afflictions of the righteous: but the LORD delivereth him out of them all", our minds quickly flee to the end of the conflict and ask the question, "When? When will this all be over?" The psalmist who penned this promise is the same psalmist who penned the complaint, "How long wilt thou forget me, O LORD? For ever? How long wilt thou hide thy face from me? How long shall I take counsel in my soul, having sorrow in my heart daily? How long shall mine enemy be exalted over me?" **(Psalms 13:1-2)** "How long wilt thou forget me, O LORD?"

King David is just like all of us, "Lord, deliver me and deliver me now!" This is where the secret of suffering becomes exciting. The reason the psalmist did not deal with the matter, sphere, concept and realm of time, is because the Holy Spirit wants to develop our faith and cause us to know and understand that we have already been delivered because of **Calvary**. This takes care of our past. We have already been delivered because of the **Comforter**. This takes care of our present. Also, we've already been delivered because **Christ is coming again.** This takes care of our future.

We have been delivered because of Calvary

Our Lord in His earthly ministry completely identified with us. There is not a feeling, fear, or physical malady that our Lord and Savior does not understand. On that cross alone, He showed us by example that He has dealt with and has overcome any peril that this world can impose upon us. Christ showed us that He has and is the answer for every human need. From the cross, Jesus uttered seven different statements; these words are comprehensive and meet every person's need. The first statement given by Jesus as He hung on the cross is found in **Luke 23:34**: "...forgive them; for they know not what they do." **Forgiveness!**

Memory is one of the greatest tormentors of life. Recollection can be an abusive bully, a relentless prosecuting attorney, and a constant reminder of our failure. The mind will collect the events of our poor choices, and our selfish acts, like a junkyard that has old relics stacked one upon the other, piled high. The video of the mind can keep people in bondage for their entire life. Guilt and self-condemnation incarcerate the soul, oppressing the spirit and opposing every movement in life. A conscience, torn by failures and regrets, causes severe depression, paralyzing the soul, making it virtually impossible for a person to have healthy thoughts about anything.

Guilt causes a disdain for life and living. You may be feeling like a failure as a husband or a father, or as a wife or a mother. Perhaps you're weighed down and burdened by many years of committing the same sin of which you are in bondage. Whatever the sin, whatever the failure, whatever the shortcoming, whatever the history may be of wrong doing, whether it be short or long, it matters not how gross, horrific, or grievous your crime against God and man may be, Jesus himself said you are forgiven if you have put your faith and trust in Him. No psychologist or psychiatrist can purge guilt. No medication or treatment can take away guilt. No worldly philosophy or educational institution can teach you how to rid yourself of guilt. No religious act, rite, work or ceremony can purge guilt from the human conscience.

No one but God can forgive sin **(Mark 2:7b)**. To say the least, guilt causes pain and suffering. How long have you been scourging your soul, tormented by guilt? How long have you allowed others to do these things to you?

One of the devil's greatest tactics is to accuse! "And I heard a loud voice saying in heaven, Now is come salvation, and strength, and the kingdom of our God, and the power of his Christ: for the accuser of the brethren is cast down, which accused them before our God day and night. And they overcame him by the blood of the Lamb, and by the word of their testimony; and they loved not their lives unto the death." **(Revelation 12:10-11)** How does one overcome guilt? "...by the blood of the Lamb..." Not only will the enemy accuse you before the throne of God night and day, but he will accuse you to yourself in your mind night and day. He does this to keep the mind in constant turmoil and pain. It has been stated that 75% of physical illness first stems from emotional maladies. Not only will the devil accuse you before God, but he will also accuse God before you.

Jesus shed His blood to forgive us of our sins. This was the penalty He paid to cleanse us and to give us a fresh new start in regeneration. We can experience the fresh new start of this forgiveness and renewal day by day. "It is of the LORD'S mercies that we are not consumed, because his compassions fail not. They are new every morning: great is thy faithfulness." **(Lamentations 3:22-23)** The Bible tells us in **1 John 1:7**, "...and the blood of Jesus Christ his Son cleanseth us from all sin." We must grow to understand the power of His blood. The blood of Christ is the very blood of God Himself **(Acts 20:24)**. His blood is holy, righteous, pure, divine, and without spot or blemish. Those who have been cleansed by faith, in the blood of Jesus Christ, have been cleansed for all time and eternity. Mental and emotional agony is the most difficult suffering of all, and our Lord wants us to be totally free from our mental and emotional bondage. It is imperative that we get an understanding and knowledge of this great truth.

Why is the shedding of the blood of Christ so powerful? The shedding of our Lord's blood is the answer to and the satisfaction of the holiness of God. God is just and completely holy **(2 Chronicles 19:7; Nehemiah 9:33; 1 Peter 1:15-16)**. His holiness and justice demands our righteousness. To enter into the holy presence of God, we must be as holy, righteous, and just as He is. Within our own human effort and self-righteousness, this is impossible. Job asks the question, "...how should a man be just with God?" **(Job 9:2)** This was a great question asked by Job. Isaiah states, "...we are all as an unclean thing, and all our righteousnesses are as filthy rags; and we all do fade as a leaf; and our iniquities, like the wind, have taken us away." **(Isaiah 64:6)** The best our efforts can produce before God is nothing more than a filthy rag.

God's perfection is unattainable by human standards. His holiness demands that sin be punished and paid for. Our Lord's death on the cross was that payment for sin. This is the very reason why God sent His Son **(John 3:17)**. God's holiness also demands justice. The justice of God was met when Jesus was brutally killed on the cross. He was God's Holy Lamb, without spot and without blemish, perfect. I do not really believe that we can understand how free we are, until we understand what it cost to really free us. When this understanding is gained and believed by faith, then freedom from our emotional bondage will be realized.

The payment of sin before a holy and righteous God is death. "... The soul that sinneth, it shall die..." **(Ezekiel 18:4, 20)** The blood of Jesus secured our redemption **(Ephesians 1:13-14),** which means we have been bought back or purchased by the Lord. That blood made possible our regeneration **(Ephesians 2:1)**. This is what it means to be born again. That blood facilitated our reconciliation **(2 Corinthians 5:18-21)**, bringing those who are in opposition together in complete unity and harmony, and guaranteed a complete remission of our sin and wrong doing **(Hebrews 9:22, 26)**. Every sin, past, present, and future has been removed and taken out of the way. Remember **1 John 1:7**: "…all sin."

> *"How much more shall the blood of Christ, who through the eternal Spirit offered himself without spot to God, purge your conscience from dead works to serve the living God?"*
>
> (HEBREWS 9:14)

This, I believe, is the most incredible verse in the Bible concerning our forgiveness of sin. We see in this verse the eternal potency of the precious blood of Christ. I believe with all my heart, as already stated, the greatest agonies endured on the planet are inner emotional conflicts. The blood of Christ, that ever-flowing river of mercy and grace, will continually cleanse the regenerated soul. Bible scholars, pastors, and teachers of the Word have so focused on the blood of Christ and its ability to cause a right standing before God by placing faith and trust in that blood, but they have failed to make plain and clear that the work of the blood and the cross of Christ can heal the damaged soul that has been eaten up with guilt and self-condemnation. The blood of Christ deals with what we do – the practice of sin. The cross of Christ deals with what we are – the personification of sin. The resurrection of Christ assures us that both the blood and the cross of Christ have accomplished in us a perfect work.

"For by one offering he hath perfected for ever them that are sanctified." **(Hebrews 10:14)** The blood and the cross of Christ have satisfied the Heavenly Father through the advocacy and work of our Savior, fulfilling the justice of the Heavenly Father's holy nature. Understanding this, we can now move to the inward working and operation of the blood and the cross of Christ within the soul. The verse we are now considering, if understood, believed and embraced, will do more for the damaged soul than any

psychologist, psychiatrist, or medication could ever hope to accomplish. In this verse, as with the whole Bible, there is a supernatural effectualness.

Notice the statement in this verse, "...purge your conscience from dead works..." **(Hebrews 9:14)** This word "purge" means to make clean, to cleanse, in both a physical and moral sense. The word picture gives us the idea of utensils being cleansed or outward diseases and physical maladies being removed. In a moral sense, this word speaks of being freed from defilement, purifying from wickedness, being made free from the guilt and condemnation of sin, consecrating or setting apart by cleansing or purifying **(Matthew 8:2-3; 10:8; 11:5; 23:25; Mark 1:40-41; Luke 5:12-13; 17:14, 17; Acts 15:9)**. The mental tormentors of guilt and self-condemnation will keep us in the solitary confinement of shame, embarrassment, and self-pity. While locked up in this torturous "death row" of conscience, one will experience nothing but a sense of worthlessness, feeling as though his or her life is just an utter failure. **Hebrews 9:14** offers a threefold truth that will forever deliver the tormented soul!

The blood of Christ has eradicated sin from the soul

The word "eradicate" means to pull up by the roots, to do away with completely. Your sin is gone, gone, gone! Our Lord has cast our sin into the deepest sea **(Micah 7:19)**. And He has separated our sin as far as the east is from the west **(Psalms 103:12)**. This type of deliverance is called being saved to the uttermost **(Hebrews 7:25)**. The psalmist put it this way, "Have mercy upon me, O God, according to thy loving kindness: according unto the multitude of thy tender mercies blot out my transgressions. Wash me thoroughly from mine iniquity, and cleanse me from all my sin." **(Psalms 51:1-2)** You've been washed, cleansed, and every sin has been blotted out! Furthermore, God will not remember your sin any longer. If the blood of Christ can do this for the memory of God, it can do it for your memory and conscience as well **(Psalms 25:7)**. Many have built memorials in their minds of their sins and failures, and then live continually within its shadows.

No such memorials should ever be built. And if so, let the blood of Christ by faith remove them all.

The blood of Christ has emancipated the soul

On September 22, 1862, Abraham Lincoln issued the Emancipation Proclamation. On January 1, 1863, the Emancipation Proclamation took full effect. This Emancipation Proclamation led to the 13th Amendment, enacted on December 18, 1865, which legally freed all slaves from bondage. These beautiful people, created by our Heavenly Father, endured 246 years of slavery. They were subjected to horrific inhumane cruelties and conditions, which are unconscionable. The depth of suffering goes beyond any description imaginable. Without these people, our nation would not be what it is today. Their invaluable contributions have helped to shape and develop our great country in every area: science, agriculture, education, ministry, politics, music, industry, the military, and sports. We have much to be thankful for as a result of their resolve and indomitable spirit.

One of the greatest characteristics exhibited by these people is that of perseverance. It would behoove us all to draw strength and wisdom from these people of influence who have touched every aspect and area of American life. Even though the Emancipation Proclamation led to the 13th Amendment, which finally and ultimately freed all the slaves, multitudes of them still lived as if they were in bondage. All of the conditions of that day were against them. Many of them had no money, no education, and nowhere to go. They had a hard time believing that the law was signed and the policy was in force. The distractions and challenges before them were great.

In like manner, Christ signed our Emancipation Proclamation and sealed it with His own blood. "Blotting out the handwriting of ordinances that was against us, which was contrary to us, and took it out of the way, nailing it to his cross..." **(Colossians 2:14)**. This means our soul has been completely emancipated, loosed, and freed. However, like the liberated slaves of old, multitudes of believers still function in fear, doubt and unbelief, serving the taskmasters of their souls and bearing the heavy burdens and chains from the former memory of their sins and failures. This type of bondage and torment can literally become a living mental hell.

In Luke, the 16th chapter, the rich man was not only physically suffering in the flames of hell but he was mentally and emotionally suffering as well. Abraham said to the rich man, "...Son, remember that thou in thy lifetime receivedst thy good things, and likewise Lazarus evil things: but now he is comforted, and thou art tormented." **(Luke 16:25)**

The emotional suffering in hell can be equivalent to the emotional suffering here on earth. However, emotional suffering here on earth can be ended. **Hebrews 9:14** shows us that the blood of Christ can be applied to the emotional suffering we experience and bring complete healing to one's soul. This whole verse talks about the healing of damaged emotions which has been ruined by the practice and experience of sin. It is that eternal Spirit that supplies the blood of Christ to the inner ruins of the heart, thus making the soul a holy, healed sanctuary for the living God.

The soul is the self-conscious part of a person (feelings, emotions, fantasies, memories and the capacity to make decisions). These intricacies make up the real person, you. This is how the Spirit of God will mend and minister to your broken spirit. The inward operation of God purges our conscience from dead works. Every vile, wretched, ugly, sinful act ever committed has been skillfully removed by the supernatural surgical scalpel of an Almighty God. When you believe this, then you'll be Free! Free! Free! To the suffering soul, I would encourage you to pray right now and say:

"Lord Jesus, I believe in the power of your blood, that it has cleansed me from every sin, past, present, and future. I ask your Holy Spirit right now to perform this operation within my soul and heal my damaged emotions. I cannot change what I have done, but I ask You to change how I feel about myself. As I trust and believe You by faith, please confirm this work within me, that I might experience your comfort, peace, and rest of soul through the ever abiding presence of your Spirit."

"For thou, Lord, art good, and ready to forgive; and plenteous in mercy unto all them that call upon thee."

(Psalms 86:5)

The blood of Christ will execute the plan and will of God within the soul

Now that the soul has been eradicated from sin and emancipated by the blood of Christ, we are free..."to serve the living God." **(Hebrews 9:14)** What a Declaration of Independence this verse is for the soul. All of the negative emotions of memory, guilt, shame, and embarrassment, which have been entombed within the conscience, has now been completely removed. All of the "dead works" of the past have been erased. The Spirit of God has regenerated, renewed, restored, replenished, and revived the soul. To be discouraged...look back. To be dejected...look within. To be distracted... look around. But to be delivered...look above.

Do not be deceived into thinking that because there is so much in your past, this now disqualifies you from serving God in the future. Or, there's more of the past and less of the future, so what's the use? Or, you may think, your past violations make you less valuable to God and inferior in the realm of His service.

If these things were true, then we would have never known the great ministry of the Apostle Paul. This man became a giant of the faith in the early church and forever more. He too struggled with the agonies of guilt and self-condemnation of the soul. I believe that Paul's thorn in the flesh could very well have been a tormented memory **(2 Corinthians 12:7)**. Why? Because before his conversion he was one of the greatest persecutors of the early church **(Galatians 1:13, 25)**. The Apostle Paul, who was also called Saul of Tarsus **(Acts 13:9)**, was present at the stoning of Stephen **(Acts 7:58; 8:1)**. I am sure that for the rest of his life, the mental pictures and images from that event often tried to haunt the memory and conscience of this dear man. He referred to himself as the chief of sinners, and "less than the least of all saints." **(1Timothy 1:15; Ephesians 3:8)**

But through divine revelation the Holy Spirit taught him the great truth of **Hebrews 9:14**, which I believe wholeheartedly God used him to pen. Listen to God's Word in another place, which God also used the Apostle Paul to write, "Brethren, I count not myself to have apprehended: but this one thing I do, forgetting those things which are behind, and reaching forth unto those things which are before, I press toward the mark for the prize of the high calling of God in Christ Jesus." **(Philippians 3:13-14)**. Did you catch that?

"FORGETTING those things which are behind..." The soul and the memory can be healed from all the dead works of the past, no matter how heinous the act. I believe the hymn writer understood this when he wrote, *"There is power, power, wonder-working power, in the blood, of the Lamb! There is power, power, wonder-working power, in the precious blood of the Lamb!"* Not only did God save Paul, but God used him to write 14 out of the 27 books of the New Testament. He started multiple churches and preached the gospel around the world **(Romans 10:18; 16:26; Colossians 1:6, 23)**. His epistles continue to evangelize even to this day. The church then, now, and forever more will feel the impact and influence of this man. His life, as well as yours, has eternal significance in the will of God **(Psalms 139:15-18; Jeremiah 1:5; Galatians 1:15; 2 Timothy 1:9)**. What made the difference for the Apostle Paul is that he believed the record God gave of His Son, concerning the sin-purging, conscience-cleansing, life-restoring power of the blood!

Our blood is ailing but HIS blood is ageless.
Our blood is blemished but HIS blood hath no blot.
Our blood is corrupt but HIS blood is cleansing.
Our blood is dead but HIS blood is divine.
Our blood is endangered but HIS blood is everlasting.
Our blood is fatigued but HIS blood is forceful.
Our blood is guilty but HIS blood is guiltless.
Our blood is hindered but HIS blood is healing.
Our blood is infirmed but HIS blood is incorruptible.
Our blood is judged but HIS blood is justified.

Our blood is kindred but HIS blood is of the King.

Our blood is lost but HIS blood is living.

Our blood is malignant but HIS blood is miraculous.

Our blood is noxious but HIS blood is noble.

Our blood is oppressed but HIS blood is omnipotent.

Our blood is polluted but HIS blood is prevailing.

Our blood is quirked but HIS blood is quickening.

Our blood is rotten but HIS blood is righteous.

Our blood is soiled but HIS blood is supernatural.

Our blood is terminal but HIS blood is triumphant.

Our blood is undone but HIS blood is unchanging.

Our blood is vile but HIS blood is victorious.

Our blood is weak but HIS blood is wonderful!

We must now return to those seven beautiful statements that Christ uttered from the cross. The second statement is found in **Luke 23:43**, "...Verily I say unto thee, today shalt thou be with me in paradise."

Fear is a great enemy of the soul, the fear of life and the fear of death. Another statement from the cross correlates and interrelates with the above. As He hung on the cross, Jesus cried out in writhing, unparalleled agony: "E-lo-i, E-lo-i La-ma Sa-bach-tha-ni?" This translates as, "My God, my God, why hast thou forsaken me?" **(Matthew 27:46)**. This third statement from the cross shows that he experienced loneliness and abandonment. These emotions cause a dread which plunge the mind into an utter chaotic state of despair. When tragedy touches our very lives (this can take on many forms), we are often left in a place of confusion, bewilderment, overwhelming sorrow and a deep depression. Job put it this way, "For the thing which I greatly feared is come upon me, and that which I was afraid of is come unto me." **(Job 3:25)** We've experienced this within our own family, through the illness and death of our son and through the tumultuous disease of cancer which afflicted our daughter.

Everything in life changes in times of severe suffering. It is common to feel that no one can understand or really know what you're going through.

The Bible, though, tells us the exact opposite of that feeling, "Beloved, think it not strange concerning the fiery trial which is to try you, as though some strange thing happened unto you:..." **(1 Peter 4:12).** The Bible also tells us that there are some burdens we can share with one another, and there are burdens which we must bear alone **(Galatians 6:2, 5).**

Conflicts, trials, sorrows, and tragedies are common threats which affect us all. Let's take a closer look at these two statements of Christ from the cross and glean some wonderful life-changing and comforting hope from them. Both of the thieves as they were being crucified with our Lord that day at first reviled him **(Matthew 27:44).** They both saw how vicious and anti-Christ the crowd was, which gathered around the cross. They both heard the vile, vociferous, blasphemous insults from multitudes of those round about the cross which hurled their verbal rocks at the object of their contempt, our precious Lord. Both thieves were suffering. Both men were bitter. And no doubt, both men had lived a life of failure and regret. But one of the two thieves acknowledged his sinfulness and need for a savior before it was eternally too late and humbled himself before the Lord.

Listen to the thief's prayer: **"...**Lord, remember me when thou comest into thy kingdom." **(Luke 23:42)** Jesus then responded by saying, "...Verily I say unto thee, today shalt thou be with me in Paradise." **(Luke 23:43)** The thief also heard the lamentation of our Lord when he said, "My God, my God, why hast thou forsaken me?" **(Matthew 27:46).** These words brought hope!

What is hope? Hope is the belief that the outcome of our present circumstances will yield rewards far greater than the pain endured. This repentant thief was suffering. His condition seemed hopeless. There was no escape from his imminent fate. He was securely fastened to the implement of his destruction. What good could come from the writhing pain of this desperate moment? The good that came was "blessed assurance." Sweet comfort from within, "And the peace of God which passeth all understanding..." **(Philippians 4:7)** He experienced the presence of God himself in the person of Jesus Christ.

What an incredible word picture we have here. When we suffer, God suffers with us. He's near, close, and right by our side. He's not aloof, detached, and unconcerned. But He is the One who will manage in great detail the bed of our affliction. In severe time of suffering, like the psalmist, we can also say, "...In thy presence is fulness of joy..." **(Psalms 16:11)**

In chapter four of 2 Timothy, the Apostle Paul lists some of his perils. He described how Demas, his friend and co-laborer in Christ, had forsaken him, and a man by the name of Alexander the coppersmith did him much evil. He declared how he had been forsaken of all men, and that he was attacked by a wild lion, but in the midst of it all, he proclaimed, "...the Lord stood with me...and I was delivered..." **(2 Timothy 4:17)** The deliverance and victory of the Lord is certain in all the adversities of life. Upon hearing the comforting words of our Lord from the cross to his soul, this dying thief would have the confidence that, "...the sufferings of this present time are not worthy to be compared with the glory which shall be revealed in us." **(Romans 8:18)**

When a suffering saint dies, what will be his or her first experience? With a heart of faith, try to put yourself in the following narrative and in so doing, may what you read next bring hope as you persevere through the trials of this life:

As I stood before the throne, beholding the beauty of His Majesty in my wonder and awe, I could not comprehend all the glorious sights. I felt as though I was alone, just God and me, but we couldn't be because I heard sounds of music: stringed instruments, percussion instruments, wind instruments—melodies so strange, progressions nothing like I had ever heard. Every note was so clear, every pitch so pure, the tones were comforting, calming, soothing, and relaxing. I heard laughter, singing, and voices of a great multitude, yet all of the sounds did not conflict or confuse. It was as if my senses could process everything harmoniously.

I felt warmth on my face which then overwhelmed my entire body. The warmth was not dry, nor was it wet, but indescribable. I felt such a sensation of safety and security. Could this be what a child experiences within the womb of its mother?

My physical being felt very strong and powerful, a strength and alertness which I have never known or experienced. I believed I could leap as high as I want, or run as fast as I desired, but I dare not move! Though I felt light and weightless, as if gravity had no power here, or could be controlled by the process of thought, I was not sure. My skin tone is not black or white, brown or yellow, but as of a color of all races, amalgamated into one beautiful scheme.

From behind the throne and out of the throne emanated the brilliancy of light, the brightness of which was greater than any sunrise or sunset, more overwhelming than the rays of the sun reflecting off a clear body of water or pure white snow. I did not have to turn my head, nor shield mine eyes from the greatness of its strength. I could gaze right upon it, and look deep into the unending depth of its glorious blaze. Just beyond the throne and the immensity of that light, I saw a multitude of colors, beams of color so radiant and beautiful, all I wanted to do was gaze intently upon them.

My gaze was fixed on this awesome wonder. My body began to tremble and shake slightly at the magnitude of this incomprehensible scene. The scope of these colors was endless, transparent like thin clear glass. The colors stretched horizontally, how far they ran I could not tell; they seem to go on forever. Then I realized what it was that I was looking at. Foundations…twelve foundations! The foundations were of jasper, sapphire, chalcedony, emerald, sardonyx, sardius, chrysolite, beryl, topaz, chrysoprasus, jacinth, and amethyst. These foundations were great, strong and mighty. I could tell that they were thick and dense, but yet you could look right through the colors, as if one could look down into a pure, still, clear pond, right down to the bottom. Although you could peer a great distance into the array, like everything else here, it was vast and seemed to have no end. I am sure that the length and width of these foundations stopped somewhere, but they were illuminated with everlasting splendor.

Then I saw twelve massive white gates with a magnificent appearance. Standing before the gates were strong, mighty, and very powerful angels. These angels were like sentinels. They stood like statuary, stoic and with a look of nobility, clothed in garments as if they were ready for battle, to defend from any foe that might unlawfully approach one of these entrances to this great city. The strength, magnitude and immeasurable weight of these gates were symbolic of the wealth and unconquerable might of the King which sits upon that omnipotent throne. This throne was the center of all the activities and structures of this indescribable place. The illumination and soft glow of these gates were iridescent, changing from beauty to beauty depending on the angle from which they were viewed. Then it came to me by direct revelation, thoughts entering my mind quickly and freely without any distractions, revealing that these gates were made of solid pearls. Their thickness and density reminded me of immovable mountainous rock! These gates of pearls are always open, as if they are saying, "Please enter. You're welcome and safe here always."

The open gates were the entrance into a magnificent city. The outside wall of this city was high, very high, over 200 feet, an impenetrable force emblematic of the eternal protection of the citizens residing therein. From a far distance, I noticed a Figure approaching me. As He drew closer, I kept my head slightly towards the ground. Then I realized the surface upon which I was standing was pure gold, yet I could look right down through it. This gold was transparent. I felt suspended in the atmosphere as I was peering right through this golden pavement. The beams of its magnificence expanded downward and outward as far as my eye could see. Like a floodlight that pierces into the darkness, then bleeds into the same, this golden array was as radiant as the glorious light which filled up this whole new universe of existence with indescribable artistry!

The voice of this Man called me by name. His words were soft, clear, and comforting. His countenance appeared gentle, compassionate, manifesting nobility and wisdom. His eyes were deep in color and His smile welcoming and hospitable. Then, He opened His arms to receive me into His bosom, and like a flash of lightning my eyes became fixed upon His hands as He continued reaching out to me like a loving father would to receive his little children. Then I saw the scars: they were sizable, conspicuous, and very difficult to look at. They were the marks of a former brutality of endured passion.

Straightway, my legs lost their ability to hold me up and I found myself plunging downwards, baptized and overwhelmed by the gravity of this experience. My tears and lamentations broke out of me with a cacophony of indiscernible sounds, like a dam which could no longer keep back the swelling floods. I was lifeless as I fell into His arms and He, bearing my entire weight, tenderly patted and rubbed my back with pure acceptance. I was reclining in the bosom of God! My face and head were pressed against and buried firmly into the strength of His embrace.

*When I felt a subtle release, I fawned, crouched, and bowed to the lowest level in worship and adoration, securely putting my arms around the bottom of His legs and resting my head like a pillow upon His feet. My tears bathed His feet, and when I had opened my eyes I saw similar scars on His feet as I did His hands. In this instant I realized Who had me in His embrace...the **Faithful Witness, the***

One which was, which is, and which is to come, the first begotten of
the dead, the Prince of the kings of the earth, the Alpha and Omega,
the beginning and the ending, the first and the last, the Almighty,
the Son of Man, the Son of God, the Savior of the world, my Lord
and my Savior. He was clothed with a garment down to His feet.
His head and hair were white like wool as white as snow. The King
of Kings and the Lord of Lords! The Lamb of God!

At this moment, I realized that I had no fear, no pain, no worries and no doubts.
The only thing that is the same here as it was on earth is the complete peace, comfort,
and joy I knew then. It is the same here and now.

The Man then touched me and gently helped me to my feet. And as I stood before
Him, profusely weeping, my face was gently nestled between His hands, and with both
of His thumbs and the palms of His hands moving from the inside out with a synchro-
nized motion, He tenderly wiped away every tear from my eyes. Then He took me in
one of His arms and held me close to His side, and with His other arm outstretched,
*He pointed at the grandeur of this imperial city of gold, and said to me, "**Well done***
thou good and faithful servant, enter thou into the joy of thy Lord!"

On one side of His cross, our compassionate Lord suffered alongside the penitent thief. On the other side, though, was the impenitent thief.
Again, here's another word picture, but a very, very, sad one. The impenitent
thief never reached out to the Lord. He never asked the Lord for forgiveness or help, though God was there the entire time. It is in the time of need
that we should flee to Christ and seek Him with all of our heart. When a
person suffers and chooses not to seek our Lord, what a tragedy it is! God
is as close as a whisper, as close as the sighing of the heart. He is ready,
He is waiting, and He is there to help. If He is not sought, called upon or
acknowledged, God's grace will seem like it is oceans away. But the moment
that first step of faith is taken, the sufferer will then plunge deep into the
refreshing waters of God's grace and help.

The words of Christ which have echoed from the cross so long ago
are a constant reminder that our Lord knew what it was like to be all alone.
In that hour, God (Christ) was forsaken of God that we might never be

forsaken of Him. We now have the wonderful promise, "I will never leave thee, nor forsake thee." **(Hebrews 13:5)** He is our guide and constant companion.

He told His disciples as well as us, "I will not leave you comfortless: I will come to you." **(John 14:18)** In this life, that thief on the cross was given hope, and that hope took him beyond the grave.

We will revisit the other words Jesus spoke on the cross. In all of these words, we will clearly see that our Lord cares for every detail and aspect of our lives. For now, take great comfort in knowing that He is a God close, especially in the time of a storm **(John 6:16-20)**. He cares and we can cast all of our care upon Him, our worries, fears, sorrows, doubts, pains, challenges, conflicts, trials, and heartaches **(1 Peter 5:7)**. He is committed to His children **(Psalms 16:2, 3; 17:8)**, and He can be called upon at any time for help **(Jeremiah 33:3)**.

CHAPTER 4

The secret of suffering is found in

IMMEASURABLE LOVE

"...Woman, behold thy son!...Behold thy mother!..."
(JOHN 19:26-27, THE FOURTH AND FIFTH STATEMENTS
FROM THE CROSS)

It is amazing that in our Lord's agonies, He was still and always thinking of others. In these statements from the cross we see the love that Jesus had for the family. His mother and His beloved closest friend, the apostle John, stood at the foot of the cross holding one another weeping as they helplessly looked on. Jesus, our great high priest, robed, blanketed, and cocooned in His own blood, looked through His swollen eyes and gave instructions as to how His mother should be cared for. The term "woman" in the Jewish culture was a term of endearment and affection. Jesus was lovingly entrusting the care of His mother to the apostle John, who would care for her the rest of her life. The love and concern that Jesus showed for His family is indicative of the love and concern He has for every family suffering and grieving. When one person in a family suffers, the whole family suffers too.

Those family dynamics can become very complex, but the love of Christ ministered by the Holy Spirit knows the exact need of every family member. The Holy Ghost will envelop the entire family in the love and care of God. He is called the "Comforter." **(John 14:26)** Later, in great detail we will explain the wonderful ministry of the Holy Spirit and how He supplies the suffering saint with everything that he or she needs, but in this section we are going to focus on His provision of the love of Christ.

Often when we suffer, we doubt. We ask the question, "Why does the Lord allow us to suffer?" The simple answer is because He loves us. Maybe I should not have made this statement so early in the book. Why? Because I don't want your thinking to turn negative. The subject of suffering has glorious implications for us. After you finish reading this book, the "why" question will dissolve.

There is much wrong thinking on the subject of suffering. For example:

1. All suffering comes from God.
2. A loving God would never allow suffering.
3. The only reason some people suffer is because of wrongdoing.
4. It is wrong for God to allow good people to suffer.

God's wisdom is vast and far beyond the comprehension of our thought. Everything He allows to come into our life, He does so because of His incredible love for us. Our Lord knows the end as well as the beginning and also everything in between. We could say that with God, everything exists in the eternal now. A biblical fact that will thrill you is found in **Hebrews 11:3**. "Through faith we understand that the worlds were framed by the word of God, so that the things which are seen were not made of things which do appear."

The word "worlds" in this verse not only speaks of the constellations or the creation of the material universe, but also refers to the matter, sphere, realm, and concept of time. The meaning is this: God has His own parenthetical statement, where your life is concerned. Within the frames of these parentheses, God is orchestrating, controlling, and managing in great detail every aspect of your life. This is true intimacy. Nothing in your life takes

God by surprise. God is overseeing the process. Nothing can come into your life, save God allows it.

Think of your life as a beautiful portrait and God is the Artist. He knows what colors to use. He knows where on the canvas of your life everything should be. Every stroke of His brush is with purpose, infallible precision, divine providence, and expression, working "...all things after the counsel of his own will:" **(Ephesians 1:11)**. After the masterpiece is completed, it is framed and hung on the wall of His eternal glory, forevermore to be viewed by the innumerable host of heaven and the great cloud of witnesses that has gone on before us **(Revelation 14:13b; Hebrews 12:1)**.

King David understood this very principle when he said, "I have set the Lord always before me: because he is at my right hand, I shall not be moved." **(Psalms 16:8)** But a conflict still exists. Here's how we play out the scenario in our thinking: If God loves me as I love my children (and of course His love surpasses that of my love), and I know that I would not allow any bad thing to harm my children, why then would God allow harm to come to His children?

Like our earthly parents, God loves His children, and has specific goals and objectives for them to attain. Suffering is a big part of God's blueprint by which He reaches the desired outcome for all of His children. "Forasmuch then as Christ hath suffered for us in the flesh, arm yourselves likewise with the same mind: for he that hath suffered in the flesh hath ceased from sin." **(1 Peter 4:1)**

Suffering makes us more Christlike. It is our need in suffering that draws us closer to our God. Suffering delivers us from carnal addictions of this world. It transcends our thinking from the natural realm to the spiritual realm, from the temporal realm to the eternal realm, from the physical realm to the supernatural realm. "While we look not at the things which are seen, but at the things which are not seen: for the things which are seen are temporal; but the things which are not seen are eternal." **(2 Corinthians 4:18)**

Suffering causes us to reach for God, seek Him, long for Him, and look for Him. When we suffer we can see Him through His providence, and we are acutely aware of His presence. In our human reason and logic, suffering would never be our plan, but logic will never solve the equation for you. For God does not move, work and function within the sphere of human reason and logic. Why? Because it is corrupt! And embraces the base tenets of earthly, fleshly thought.

We must study and contemplate the following verses:

- *"For the wisdom of this world is foolishness with God. For it is written, he taketh the wise in their own craftiness."* **(1 Corinthians 3:19)**
  - o *Craftiness: this is a suspicious or false wisdom. Pretense. This is why man accuses God, blames God, and comes to the very false conclusion that "God must be angry with me or hates me, this is why the severity of illness or conflict has come upon me."*
- *"For our rejoicing is this, the testimony of our conscience, that in simplicity and Godly sincerity, not with fleshly wisdom, but by the grace of God, we have had our conversation in the world, and more abundantly to you-ward." (2 Corinthians 1:12)*
  - o *Fleshly: sinful, carnal, and influenced by deception.*
- *"For it is written, I will destroy the wisdom of the wise, and will bring to nothing the understanding of the prudent. Where is the wise? Where is the scribe? Where is the disputer of this world? Hath not God made foolish the wisdom of this world? For after that in the wisdom of God the world by wisdom knew not God? It pleased God by the foolishness of preaching to save them that believe."* **(1 Corinthians 1:19-21)**
  - o *Destroy: man's wisdom, logic, and human reasoning led to the rejection of Christ and causes people to continue to walk in darkness. One day, this too will finally and ultimately be judged by God.*
  - o *Nothing:* our reasoning and logic has no value.
    "Howbeit we speak wisdom among them that are perfect:

yet not the wisdom of this world, nor of the princes of this world, that come to naught." **(1 Corinthians 2:6)**

There are two more supporting texts that will help us to understand that God does not think as we do: "for my thoughts are not your thoughts, neither are your ways my ways, saith the Lord. For as the heavens are higher than the earth, so are my ways higher than your ways, and my thoughts than your thoughts." **(Isaiah 55:8-9)** "O the depth of the riches both of the wisdom and knowledge of God! How unsearchable are his judgments, and his ways past finding out!" **(Romans 11:33)**

It is clear by the above verses that our philosophy, human reasoning, and logic has no good place or standing before the infallible purposes of God. The world's wisdom as described by God's Word is foolishness.

I don't want to seem harsh or cruel at this point. One of the most recurring truths of the Bible is that God desires for His people to see things and view things in the way that He does. For 36 chapters, Job laments, questions and contends with God, manifesting deep hurt, bitterness, and sorrow. When he stopped talking, and God finally spoke, He did not answer the question of why. He just calmly said to Job, let Me explain to you Who I am! And when God finished His dialogue, Job simply responded by saying: Lord, you can give counsel without knowledge. Meaning, Lord you do not have to explain yourself to me, I get it! And Job finally came to realize and understand why. God simply wanted Job to trust Him. To trust His plan, His wisdom, and His love for Job. Job went on to say about God, that His ways went far beyond Job's process of thought, "I understood not, things too wonderful for me, which I knew not." **(Job 42:3b)** "I have heard of thee by the hearing of the ear: but now mine eyes seeth thee. Wherefore I abhor myself, and repent in dust and ashes." **(Job 42:5-6)**

This following story was told by Edwin M. Kerlin. Dr. G.F. Pentecost was once trying to comfort a woman who had passed through sore trials. Failing in his efforts to cheer her and dispel her doubts, he took up some embroidery upon which she had been working and said, "What a confusion of threads! Why waste time on a thing like that?" Turning the embroidery over, she said, "Now look at it. You were seeing it from the wrong side." "That's it, exactly," said Dr. Pentecost. "You are looking at your trials from the wrong side. Turn them over and look at them from the right side–that is, from God's side. The Lord is working out a design of His own for your life, and you must look at things from His point of view, and trust His workmanship."

God's love for His children is immeasurable, unparalleled, eternal, and inexhaustible. He wants us to simply trust Him for everything in our life, without reservation or apprehension, "Casting all your care upon him; for he cares for you." **(1 Peter 5:7)** How much does God love you?

One of the greatest — if not the greatest — verse in the Bible declares, "For God so loved the world, that he gave his only begotten son, that whosoever believeth in him should not perish, but have everlasting life." **(John 3:16)** What a declaration of love this is. This verse demonstrates the height, depth, length, breadth, and scope of God's demonstrative love, which goes beyond our comprehension, process of thought, and ability for articulation. His love is like a well without bottom, an ocean without end, and a beam of light which shines into eternity! Many aspects of God's love is taught in this verse:

- **For God - that is the source of love**
- **so loved - that is stupendous love**
- **the world - the sinners He loves**
- **that He gave - this is the sacrifice of love**
- **His only begotten son - that's sacred love**
- **that whosoever believeth in Him - this is the simplicity of love**
- **should not perish but have everlasting life - that's the security of love**

The only word we have to delineate, describe, and define the love of God according to **John 3:16** is found in the little word – "so." I mean no irreverence by this next written statement: not even the Holy Spirit Himself, could completely define in words the magnitude of God's inexhaustible love! All He, the Holy Spirit, could do was use the little word – "so." This word reaches into eternity and has no visible boundary. Let me try to explain this little word – "so." After our Lord was arrested in the Garden of Gethsemane, He stood and went through seven false trials of mockery.

First, He stood before Annas, the high priest **John 18:13**. Then He stood before Caiaphas, the high priest **John 18:24**. From there He was taken to stand before the Sanhedrin court **(Mark 15:1; Luke 22:66-71)**. After that He stood before Pilate, and from Pilate to Herod, then from Herod back to Pilate, and from Pilate He was handed over to the Roman soldiers, and from the Roman soldiers He was placed upon the cross **(Luke 23:1-4; 7-12; Matthew 27:27-37)**. All during this time our Lord was brutalized and entreated very cruelly. He was beaten with a whip embedded with bone, stone and glass. They baptized and covered His face with spit: brown spit, green spit, yellow spit, vile spit! They platted a crown of thorns that dug into His skull. They blindfolded and repeatedly struck and punched His precious face. The prophet Isaiah said, "As many were astonied at thee; his visage was so marred more than any man, and his form more than the sons of men." **(Isaiah 52:14)** Before Christ ever went to the cross He was a mass of unsightly quivering flesh. He was unrecognizable! In addition to this, He was stripped naked and publicly humiliated. Jesus did not give up, He did not quit, He did not fall by the wayside. He did not stop. Why? Because you were His desire, purpose, mission, and focus. He did not give up because *He so loved you!*

Then they led Him to Calvary. Bearing His cross, He finally came to that place called Golgotha. He was laid upon that implement of torture, the cruel Roman cross. The Roman soldiers drove the spikes through His hands and His feet and then suspended His body between heaven and earth. For six agonizing hours our Lord hung on that cross, exposed to the principalities and powers, to the rulers of the darkness of this world, to spiritual wickedness in high places **(Ephesians 6:12)**. The enemy with his evil and darkness shredded His body. And there He was hanging, hopeless, helpless, and all alone.

But He did not quit; He did not cease; He did not give up; He did not stop; He did not fall by the wayside. Why? Because you were His purpose, desire, mission and focus – He so loved you.

In the sixth statement from the cross we get a glimpse into the depth of His sufferings and agonies which also reveals the unending depth of His love: "I thirst." **(John 19:28)** This great lament echoes through the centuries, revealing the depths of Christ's infirmities and distress. Beholding the suffering of Christ, we don't need to thirst for understanding and answers. We can recline in the bosom of His love and listen to His heart as it beats in affection for us. Jesus knows suffering and He knows how to succour (help, relief, aid or assist) His children who are suffering. Why? Because He "so loved you." To know the love of Christ in the midst of your suffering, or to know that you are "so loved" *of* God, should help put in perspective His desire and care for you and your family.

The last and final statements that Jesus uttered from the cross has in it for us a provocative and insightful truth concerning the accomplishment of our suffering: "And when Jesus had cried with a loud voice, he said, father, into thy hands I commend my spirit..." **(Luke 23:46)** "... It is finished..." **(John 19:30)**

Jesus knows the beginning and the end of the conflict. The Heavenly Father had a divine purpose for the suffering of His Son. He also has a divine purpose in all of our sufferings. There is a beginning and there is an end. During the process, He is in complete control and will manage every detail. In our sufferings, the supernatural God is doing His supernatural work.

This is so evident as you observe the earthly life of Christ with all of His challenges, conflicts, trials and sufferings. From our Lord's conception to His cross, His Heavenly Father was intimately involved and providentially had a part in every detail and aspect of every event in His life. When it comes to our suffering God will one day say, "It is finished." From the conception of your trials to the conclusion of your trials you can have the blessed assurance that God is managing the process. When the Apostle Paul reflected on his life and ministry of many, many trials, he was able to say with confidence concerning the involvement of his God, "And the Lord stood with me." **(2 Timothy 4:17)**

- Contemplating the depth of God's suffering helps us to understand that He completely understands and identifies with the depth of our suffering. He is not far away from us or ignoring us in our suffering, or that of our family. The fact that Jesus' mother, the Apostle John, and Jesus were all suffering together on that hill, is a beautiful illustration that God through the agent of the Holy Spirit is suffering right alongside of you and your family!

CHAPTER 5

The secret of suffering is found in

INTIMATE LOVE

O nly through the sacrifice of Christ could God exhibit the intimacy of His love. For more than thirty years, I contemplated the purpose of the ugliness and brutalities of the cross. The answer to this question shows us what suffering can accomplish in our lives. This puts us in a unique position, because in Christ's suffering we are exposed to the knowledge and understanding that the giving of Himself caused Him suffering. He abandoned His own will to express to us the greatness of His love: "Not my will, but thine, be done." **(Luke 22:42)**

Let me explain: omnipotence, omniscience, omnipresence, immutability, and infallibility could be comprehended by man from the dawn of creation. But the mystery of love could not be revealed or manifested except through sacrifice. Before the fall, God could have implanted such knowledge within the mind of man, but this would have negated the exercise of man's free will towards God. The only way that God could have exhibited His love, and God is love **(1 John 4:7-8),** was through the giving and sacrificing of His Son, the giving of Himself! This was the only way that His marvelous grace could be revealed, understood, or comprehended by man.

Only in redemption could the following moral attributes of God be experienced: mercy, grace, loving-kindness, forbearance, long-suffering, holiness, and forgiveness. Now we can understand "...The mystery of His will..." **(Ephesians 1:9)**, "...The mystery of Christ..." **(Ephesians 3:4)**, "...The Fellowship of the mystery..." **(Ephesians 3:9)**, "...The mystery of the gospel..." **(Ephesians 6:19)**, "...The mystery of iniquity..." **(2 Thessalonians 2:7)**, "... And the revelation of the mystery, which was kept secret since the world began..." **(Romans 16:25)**

God did not will Adam to sin, but He knew Adam would sin. God did not destroy Adam on the spot because Adam was created in the image and likeness of God **(Genesis 1:26)**. God would thus be destroying a part of Himself. This is the uniqueness and intimacy of our creation, and an element which made our redemption a necessary purpose in the plan of God **(Ephesians 3:11)**. For this reason God in Christ Jesus would subject Himself to the brutalities, cruelties, and wickedness of this sin-cursed world. This is the only way we would have ever known "...the fullness of the blessing of the gospel of Christ." **(Romans 15:29)** Therefore "...Christ was the Lamb slain from the foundation of the world..." **(Revelation 13:8)** So that in the cross we would be able to comprehend the intimacy of His love and marvelous grace, which otherwise we would have never known.

When we suffer, we are given the opportunity to love our Lord in this self-same manner. This is how we will begin to realize the supernatural presence of God enveloping our lives. When we do this, we will see some things, know some things, understand some things, and experience some things that otherwise we would have never seen, known, understood, or experienced had God not allowed us to go through suffering.

I am not writing this from a position of speculation, conjecture, or assumption but from experience. Our experiences do not dictate doctrine, but pure Bible doctrine validates and authenticates our experiences with God as genuine. On November 14, 1998, my wife went into labor after carrying our baby full-term. Her pregnancy was a healthy pregnancy with no apparent or imminent risk. That night in the delivery room something went radically wrong. I recall the doctor looking at me with panic in his eyes. He said in a very nervous voice, "We've got to get this baby out of her."

It was a tumultuous, heart-wrenching process, watching my wife labor vigorously and tirelessly as a result of a never-ending strain of constant contractions, and viewing the medical staff present as they hurried about their duties nervously. Their body language spoke negatively concerning the imminent outcome of this birth. Finally, when our baby was born he was surrounded by a medical team which feverishly worked to keep him alive.

"Tiger B." (that was my nickname for the little guy) was rushed off to the intensive care unit. The six months which would follow was the most life-changing, life-altering experience I would ever know. Our little baby boy went through more medically in six months, than many would in three lifetimes. Day after day and night after sleepless night I recall sitting in the intensive care unit at the hospital with our little son and my wife, all the while viewing his little body hooked up to all those wires and tubes which led to the different machines, which at that time were sustaining his life. He was born having experienced severe air deprivation.

One of the most difficult parts for me was hearing the screams of my son resulting from his agonizing pain. This left me feeling helpless and hopeless because I could do nothing to alter or change our circumstance. I begged God to allow me to trade places, my life for his. I would have gladly taken all of his pain and affliction in his stead. In that very moment our Lord reminded me that He gave His only Son who did take my place, my sin, and my eternal affliction. Though God would soon reveal many more truths to me, He was silent when it came to my request, supplication, and the earnest desire that my son would be healed and relieved from his pain.

Every day we hoped for a miracle, but none came. What did occur, though, was three surgeries for cut-down I.V.s, two blood transfusions, and a surgery to insert a feeding tube into his stomach, due to his inability to suck and swallow because of the damage to his brain. His natural intuition and reflex to suck was not functioning. How many people would think of such a small matter as that? We never did until it happened to us. God reminded me again that even the smallest most insignificant things, we should be thankful for. Every time I see a little baby breast-feeding, drinking from a bottle, or sucking a pacifier, I give God thanks for the ability He has given that little one. In our son, this was broken. It didn't work, and God never answered my prayer in the way I desired it to be answered. "Lord, please allow my son to suck on his own so the feeding tube could be removed." From God...silence. The feeding tube was never removed.

Many more prayers were prayed: "Lord, please allow our son to breathe on his own without a ventilator." From God...silence. The ventilator was never removed. "Lord, please remove the mucus and fluid buildup, so he won't drown and choke." The mucus and the fluid restricted his airwaves and accumulated in his lungs. To help him breathe and keep him alive, we would have to run a small tube through his nose and down his throat to clear out his airway. Often this had to be done every 15 or 20 minutes. Also, we had to perform a procedure called percussion treatments, by using a small soft rubber instrument that you can hold in your hand. This would be used to tap repeatedly with enough pressure and force on the chest area and the upper back to loosen fluid buildup in his lungs. His little body could only take so much pounding. This exercise was also necessary to keep our son alive.

I remember the doctor telling me, "You must give his little body a break, for it cannot sustain percussion treatments continually." It's a very precarious position to be in, having to pound on your son's body just to keep him alive. From God...silence.

This process never stopped until Tiger B. went to heaven. This was our life, every minute of every day, around the clock. In addition, I had to watch my other four children suffer along with my wife as a result of this tragedy. Our family was completely ravaged. Trips to the hospital seemed endless. Frequent visits to our home by doctors, social workers, physical therapists, hospice volunteers, and overnight nurses was our daily routine.

Our household was in a constant state of turmoil and interruption. Every aspect of our lives was filled with stress. As a result of the medical bills, my wife and I experienced complete financial devastation.

I never stopped trusting, hoping, and crying out to God. During this time I made a covenant with God, no deals, just a promise. I said to our Lord, "If You choose to heal my son, I will continue to love You, honor

You, serve You, worship You, and live for You. If You desire to leave him maimed and sick, I will do the same. If in Your infallible wisdom and perfect will You choose to take my son to heaven, I will also do the same: love, honor, serve, worship and live for you!"

God allowed me, and put me in a position, to return to Him the intimacy of my love for Him through suffering as He did for me. Though this was the darkest hour of my life, it was the most intimate time of communion and revelation from God I have ever known.

Another amazing truth I want to share with you concerning God's intimate love, is how it will remove all fear from our life. Suffering, illness, disease, the fear of the unknown, and tragedies can all cause and grip our soul with fear.

We read in **1 John 4:18,** *"There is no fear in love; but perfect love casteth out fear: because fear hath torment. He that feareth is not made perfect in love."*

Wow, did you see that? "There is no fear in love..." This is very interesting language. Notice, the Apostle John did not say through divine inspiration there is no fear in God's power, or, there is no fear in God's almightiness. Nor did he say, there is no fear in God's sovereignty. Furthermore, he did not say there is no fear in God's greatness. I'm sure you've heard the youthful boast when kids say, "my daddy is stronger than your daddy, and my daddy can beat up your daddy."

Let's consider these two dads. The name of the one dad is fear, and the name of the other dad is love. Now, would it not sound more reasonable to you if the latter dad's name was power, almightiness, sovereignty, or greatness? Those names certainly convey the attributes and characteristics of strength and might, do they not? Surely you would think those attributes would undoubtedly result in the easy defeat of fear. But these are not the expressions God used. He said that His love would remove all fear. It took me more than ten years to understand this truth.

When God finally revealed it to me it caused great rejoicing in my soul from that point on. God's love will dispel all of our fears. When the understanding of this falls on us, it will change our lives forever, and cause us to be fearless. God is trying to get us to recognize a great truth about Him.

John 4:18 is explained in **John 17:23**. This is our Lord's high priestly prayer. "I in them, and thou in me, that they may be made perfect in one; and that the world may know that thou hast sent me, and hast loved them, as thou hast loved me." Here we see one of the most incredible truths of God's Word, and if you will, by faith, just believe and embrace this one incredible fact, your life will be free from all fear. In this prayer, Jesus asked His Heavenly Father to supernaturally reveal to His disciples (His children - that's you and I) that they are loved by God the Father, just as much as God the Father loves His Son, Jesus. "That thou...hast loved them, as thou hast loved me." This bears repeating. Jesus is teaching us that His Heavenly Father loves you just as much as He loves His Son, Jesus! Praise the Lord, glory to God, hallelujah, blessed be to His holy name!

You protect, care, nurture, watch over, and provide for the objects of your love: your family, friends, and the people you care about. God is the same, but far beyond us in all these areas. We are the apple of His eye **(Psalms 17:8)**. We are His excellent ones in "...whom is all my delight" **(Psalms 16:3)** His little children **(John 21:5)**. Our Heavenly Father views us as kings and priests **(Revelation 1:6)**. There is no greater love than that of a father or mother for their children. Yet the love of our Heavenly Father is incomparable, incomprehensible, inconceivable, and unparalleled.

When you realize, recognize, and believe that you are loved of your Heavenly Father as much as He loves His Son, Jesus, this understanding will then remove all fear from your life. This is why God said in His Word, "there is no fear in love." **(1 John 4:18)** This knowledge will strengthen you from within, and will help keep your mind from confusion and anxiety. "For God hath not given us the spirit of fear; but of power, and of love, and of a sound mind." **(2 Timothy 1:7)**

CHAPTER 6

The secret of suffering is found

WHEN GOD IS SILENT

"... He answered her not a word..."

(MATTHEW 15:23)

I have sat with many suffering saints who in their misery have asked the unanswerable and mysterious questions, "Why is God not answering my prayers?" "How long must I go through this affliction?" "Where is God in all this?" "Why does He seem so far away?" "Why won't He reveal to me why these things are happening?"

In **Matthew 15:21-28** we meet a grieving, suffering, concerned mother. We know her as the Canaanite woman. The Canaanite religion was a system of idolatry. She lived under the Roman empire, which at that time worshiped more than 33,000 false gods. The first important thing to mention here is that Jesus went out of His way some thirty miles to have an encounter with this Canaanite woman. He knew she was there, and He also knew she was a woman in great need. Furthermore, the Lord had a perfect purpose and plan already established for this woman's life. Everything Jesus did in His earthly ministry was with order and design. God knows where you are and He will come to you in the midst of your storm **(Matthew 14:25; Mark 6:48; John 6:19-20)**.

In this narration you will notice that her daughter "...was grievously vexed with a devil." **(Matthew 15:22)** This woman's heathenism and false polytheistic observances, no doubt, exposed her daughter to satanic oppression and possession. Before her encounter with Jesus, this woman had probably tried everything the world could offer to save her child with no success. The medical practice of her day failed, the secular humanism of that time failed, the numerous philosophies and explanations offered by the Roman Empire failed, and the thousands of false deities had failed this exasperated mother.

In this account we find her rushing into the presence of God and making her plea, "Have mercy on me, O Lord, thou son of David; my daughter is grievously vexed with a devil." **(Matthew 15:22)** By recognizing Him as Lord, she appealed to His sovereignty and His power. By acknowledging Him as the Son of David she appealed to His kingly authority. She obviously came to the conclusion and belief that Jesus was the Son of God, the Savior of the world. She brought her plight to the Lord: her suffering, grief, pain, anxieties, concerns and all her worries.

In **Matthew 15:21-27,** the Bible records she "cried unto him." Notice our Lord's response: "He answered her not a word..." Heaven was silent and non-responsive. This was rejection number one. Now it gets worse. Our Lord's disciples, the so-called men of God, the people of the church, now reject her. Listen to their words: "His disciples came and besought him, saying, send her away; for she crieth after us." Here is rejection number two. Hold on, there is more bad news to come. Jesus responds to His disciples in the presence of this woman. She can hear everything that's going on: "but he answered and said, I am not sent but unto the lost sheep of the house of Israel." Blazing, glaring rejection number three!

You would think after three rejections she would have stomped out of the presence of Christ, calling Him names, blaming Him for not listening, for not acknowledging her, or being willing to help her. She did not leave and go back to her circle of family and friends and complain to them about how rude and nasty she was treated by the disciples and the church. She did not give up or quit pursuing God. Her resolve was remarkable and steadfast. What did she do? "Then came she and worshiped him, saying, Lord, help me."

This woman, in the midst of her trials, agonies, and affliction, did not become bitter at God, nor would she stop seeking Him. After being rejected three times, shunned and pushed away, she came to Christ and humbled herself. She worshiped! She sought and experienced intimacy with God. When we talk to God, as this woman did, it is then that we will get close to Him. Often, like this dear lady, we run into the presence of God with a great need and say, "Me, me, me. My, my, my. Give me, give me, give me." God often gets looked upon like a magic wand, a spare tire, a microwave, or an antibiotic solution. "I want what I want, and I want it now."

When we take time to worship in the midst of our trials and have fellowship with God, this exercises and strengthens our faith, as it did for this suffering mother. By worshiping God as we go through our conflicts, we keep ourselves in the presence of God. This allows Him to reveal Himself to us. When this takes place, it builds a confidence, intimacy, and fellowship that cannot be experienced outside the realm of suffering. She "worshiped him," says so much about her character, faith, and trust in God. By worshiping Him, she was saying that she was committed to resting, believing, and waiting on Him for everything.

I believe wholeheartedly this event influenced the apostle Peter to write later in his life these inspired words, "Casting all your care upon him; for he careth for you." **(1 Peter 5:7)** It is need that drives us to God, and it was a great need in this mother's life that drove her to seek the living God.

Recognize this woman's **perseverance**. Right in the midst of her worshiping, intense supplication, and the utterance of her broken heart and spirit she moaned, "Help me." Our Lord now delivers the fourth and crushing blow, "It is not meet to take the children's bread, and cast it to dogs." Yeah. You heard Him right. He said dogs. He called her people and everything associated with them — lifestyle, philosophy, and religion — dogs. What do you think she did next? She continued to seek God and to humble herself before Almighty God.

This woman, I believe, is one of the greatest, if not the greatest examples of faith that we find in all of the Word of God. Ten John Deere tractors and five Mack trucks could not pull this woman away from the pursuit of her God! What we see in this spectacular woman is a complete self-effacement and abandoning of her own will in order to know and experience God's will for her life. Listen to her response: "And she said, truth, Lord: yet the dogs eat of the crumbs which fall from their masters' table." This is perhaps one of the most remarkable statements that we find in the Bible.

I want to talk about the little word "yet" that she used. Through her tears, crying, groaning, and lamentation she was telling our Lord she had nowhere else to go. My friend, this is exactly the place where God desires all of us to be in our life. Depending on and seeking Him for everything. Every aspect and area of life can fail you, but God never will. Her family, friends, religion, doctors, and wealth could not help her. Her exemplary faith is shown in her **proclamation**, "... The dogs eat of the crumbs which fall from their masters' table." This believing, grieving, suffering, and desperate mother persevered not through one, but four blatant rejections. Her faith was such that she announced loudly, I'm not asking you for the bread! She knew that Jesus was the Bread of Life **(John 6:48)**. The disciples had the Bread of Life with them at all times yet did not recognize Him. She demonstratively exclaimed, "I am not asking you for the bread, for I believe that the crumbs of your power is sufficient enough to meet my need!"

To that I say, "Wow!" And so did Jesus! For He said to her and of her, "O woman, great is thy faith: be it unto thee even as thou wilt." Our Lord, handed this lady an empty check, and said, "Ma'am, you fill it in." What did the Canaanite woman do in the midst of her storm? It's amazing to me that she asked none of the questions of our Lord that we outlined at the beginning of this chapter. I am not saying those questions are sinful or wrong, but what I am saying is that her faith was able to look beyond all of those questions. Here's what she did:

- She believed in God even beyond the difficult circumstances of her life.

- Her faith and focus kept her from becoming bitter.
- She refused to allow the outward circumstances to distract her.
- She did not blame anyone for her suffering, not even herself.
- Throughout the conflict she kept herself in the spiritual realm and kept herself from the natural, tangible, and physical realm.
- She refused to give up.
- She had great expectation of what God would do. She was able to see the end of the battle, and believed herself in Christ to be victorious.

What do we learn in this story about the perspective of God?

- God knows and is aware of our conflicts, trials, and afflictions.
- He cares and will come to us in our time of need.
- His ways are perfect, though we may not understand them.
- His silence does not mean inactivity or lack of involvement.
- God's timing is perfect.
- His children bring Him glory when they diligently seek Him through their sufferings.
- He uses our trials to teach the world and the church about His grace and power.
- He always has an end result in mind and it is always for our good.

The true story of Joseph is another great biblical example of how God moves and works in the lives of His children even though they may not be able to see Him. You can read about Joseph, in **Genesis Chapters 37 and 39-50**. When Joseph was seventeen years old, he was seized by his ten older brothers. They stripped him of his coat of many colors and they threw him into a deep pit. Ignoring his pleas and cries for mercy, their plan was to leave him there to die. When Joseph's brothers saw a band of Ishmaelites approaching them, they changed their mind and decided to sell Joseph to them as a slave. Then Joseph was carried away into the land of Egypt.

In Egypt, he was sold by the Midianites to a man by the name of

Potiphar. Potiphar was an officer of Pharaoh, and a captain of his guard. While serving as the chief steward in Potiphar's house, Joseph was daily harassed by the sexual advances of Potiphar's wife. Time and time again Joseph would flee from that temptation and would not allow that evil to befall him. Potiphar's wife, scorned by this rejection, falsely accused Joseph of attempting to rape her. When Potiphar heard the lies told by his wife concerning Joseph, he was filled with wrath and anger and had Joseph thrust into Pharaoh's prison. One can only imagine the weight of Joseph's fear, anxiety, feelings of betrayal, abandonment, loneliness, and confusion after having been separated from his family for over twenty years.

After two years in prison, Joseph was released because he was able, by God's grace, to interpret Pharaoh's dream when no one else could. Pharaoh was so impressed by the good character and talent of Joseph that he elevated him to a place of second in command over the entire Egyptian Empire.

Where was God in all this? From the protection of his father's house, to the disparity of that deep pit, through the disparagement and defamation brought upon him by Potiphar's wife, having experienced the dejection of doing prison time though innocent, God's Word emphatically tells us that Joseph was never alone: "And the Lord was with Joseph...but the Lord was with Joseph..." **(Genesis 39:2, 21)**

As we continue to consider the story of Joseph, I want to take you on an imaginary journey. What if God had appeared to Joseph the very moment he was thrown into that horrible pit, and at that extremely fearful time gave to him the immediate answers of "why" concerning this dreadful experience?

"Joseph, you're going to be okay. I am working everything out, overseeing and managing every detail. Here's how the process will work. Very soon you're going to be sold into slavery and become a servant to a man by the name of Potiphar. During your tenure there, Potiphar's wife will make many illicit sexual advances towards you. I know you are faithful, Joseph, and you love Me very much, therefore, you will reject her every time. Because of this stand for righteousness, you'll be entrapped, falsely accused by this

wicked woman, and thrown into a nasty prison. This will become one of the lowest periods of your life.

The next thing I will do is orchestrate the arrest of the King's cupbearer and chief baker. These two men will be cast into the same prison with you. Both the cupbearer and chief baker will have disturbing dreams, which you, Joseph, will interpret. You're going to cut a deal with these guys and ask of them upon their release to bring your cause and case before the Pharaoh, so that you also may be acquitted. The next thing that will happen, Joseph, is that these guys will forget all about you. The chief baker will disobey the Pharaoh and have his head removed. The King's cupbearer will be restored to his duties and will not think about you for another two years. At this two-year mark I'm going to cause the Pharaoh to have a very bad dream. No one in the Egyptian Empire will be able to interpret his dream. Pharaoh's cupbearer will then remember your gift and talent for interpreting dreams. He will tell the panic-stricken, hyperventilating Pharaoh all about you. Then you will be released from prison and brought before Pharaoh. Joseph, you will be the only one who can interpret his dream. Pharaoh will be so impressed with your God-given ability and great wisdom that he will exalt you to a place of preeminence in his empire.

Joseph, you will become the second most powerful man in the world! I allowed all of this to happen to you, Joseph, so that through you, I could save the world and your family from starvation. I will bring your family into Egypt, and your posterity will grow into the millions. Your people will become a great nation, all starting with your father. Egypt will enslave your people for over 400 years. I will raise up a man by the name of Moses, to whom I will give great power and ability.

Through Moses, I will perform ten mighty miracles and will completely defeat the Egyptians. Moses will then lead your people to the land I have promised. This land will be flowing with milk and honey. I will establish them there as my nation called after the name of your father, Israel. My nation will be hated by all the other nations.

Joseph, through your people and My nation I will send my Son, Jesus, who will be the Savior of the world! Furthermore, your story, Joseph, will be recorded in my Word and you will bless and affect the lives of billions of people. Joseph, you will become one of the greatest icons and legends of world history. What you will accomplish through your suffering will be remembered for all of eternity!"

If Joseph would have known all of this up front, what need would there have been for faith, hope, dependence on God, the power of His grace, and the seeking of His face? In applying this truth to our own life, as it relates to suffering, we would forfeit our need to seek Him diligently, a seeking that creates closeness, intimacy, fellowship, a communion, and a unique relationship with the Heavenly Father. Having omniscience in the area of suffering would dethrone God in our thinking. Those who are the closest to the Lord are those who have suffered the most, because in the time of suffering, they have aggressively pursued and found a beautiful revelation of Him. If we never knew the deep valley of suffering, we could never experience the mountaintop of sweet victory.

If God answered every question, would you be satisfied? Would you be content in knowing? After reading this chapter, if your answer is "yes," I do not fault, condemn, nor judge you. Though, I do not know the depth of your sorrow and suffering, I would only challenge you with this thought: If God would reveal all to you, then you would be disqualified from great reward and from knowing God's most excellent way for your life. Your desire for knowing can supersede your faith, robbing you of wonderful experiences with God. "...But we glory in tribulations also: knowing that tribulation worketh patience; and patience, experience; and experience, hope: And hope maketh not ashamed; because the love of God is shed abroad in our hearts by the Holy Ghost which is given unto us." **(Romans 5:3-5)** If God revealed everything to us prior to going into a trial, He would only be disseminating information, and we would never know intimacy with Him.

Suffering has purpose. "And we know that all things work together for good to them that love God, to them who are the called according to his purpose." **(Romans 8:28)** Suffering has a destiny to fulfill. "That I may know him, and the power of his resurrection, and the fellowship of his sufferings, being made conformable unto his death." **(Philippians 3:10)** Suffering in faith has eternal implications. "Blessed are the dead which die in the Lord, from henceforth: yea saith the Spirit, that they may rest from their labors; and their works do follow them." **(Revelation 14:13)**

Sin is the cause of all suffering, and that suffering has an enduring effect. However, when we face our suffering with faithfulness, we are commended by our Heavenly Father and will reap eternal rewards. God's heart is most fully known and revealed through sufferings. From the time of the fall to the present, suffering that acknowledges and proclaims love for the Father is perhaps the greatest gift which our free moral choice can offer Him **(Hebrews 13:15)**.

Showing devotion during a time of devastation is the highest form of praise which can be offered to our Savior! One day we shall not only be rewarded for our faith and obedience, but also for our obedience of faith as we persevered in love for our Master through suffering. Suffering is a necessary reality in our Christian journey. It was prophetically ordained before the foundations of the world in the eternal past. The Word of God, which is just as eternal as God Himself, had recorded in Its non-tangible state, the many instances and occurrences of extreme suffering and even martyrdom of God's children. **Psalms 119:89** declares, "for ever, O Lord, thy word is settled in heaven." Everything that takes place was foreseen by the omniscience of God, His all-knowing predetermined events. Therefore, His expected end has glorious implications for the suffering saints throughout all the dispensations of time: "For I know the thoughts that I think toward you, saith the Lord, thoughts of peace, and not of evil, to give you an expected end." **(Jeremiah 29:11)**

Our challenge is not to figure out why we are suffering, but to fulfill our destiny which He has prepared for us through suffering. The moment in time when our suffering exists is but a grain of sand in comparison to the universe of His glories which shall be revealed in us, "for I reckon that the sufferings of this present time are not worthy to be compared with the glory which shall be revealed in us." **(Romans 8:18)** Every suffering saint has been entrusted with this assignment: "That no man should be moved by these afflictions: for yourselves know that we were appointed thereunto" **(1 Thessalonians 3:3)**.

We are implored to follow in the footsteps of Jesus, and pattern our life of suffering after the example which He set, "for even hereunto were ye called: because Christ also suffered for us, leaving us an example, that ye should follow his steps." **(1 Peter 2:21)**

CHAPTER 7

The secret of suffering is found in

THE ATTITUDE OF FAITH

"If we cannot change the situation, we can change our attitude, by adopting the attitude of faith."

"Now the God of hope fill you with all joy and peace in believing, that ye may abound in hope, through the power of the Holy Ghost."

(ROMANS 15:13)

Our whole Christian system is built on faith. The foundation, rock, pillar, shield, cornerstone and high-tower of our hope is our faith in Christ. As a portrait is balanced on the wall hanging upon a nail, so does all of the weight of our faith rest upon Christ. Without faith, we cannot have hope, peace, comfort, joy or the blessed experience of the presence of God with us in our time of suffering.

Faith is to the soul, what a drink of water is to a dehydrated body. Our text above tells us that the God of hope will fill us "...With all joy and peace..." but this benefit does not take effect unless we believe. Notice the next phrase, "...In believing, that ye may abound in hope..." When we believe, all these wonderful graces and virtues are activated; without belief we are empty and barren. Faith unleashes the supernatural quality of being into our state of existence, which flows only from the Godhead. Faith is the conduit through which the properties and agents of God's peace, comfort, mercy, grace, joy, and blessings flow.

We must now define faith and hope. First, let's start with the word **FAITH**. "Now faith is the substance of things hoped for, the evidence of things not seen." **(Hebrews 11:1)** Faith is not a life of fatalism, nor is it a walk in the dark. Faith is a walk in the light of the Word of God. "Thy word is a lamp unto my feet, and a light unto my path." **(Psalms 119:105)** Faith is stepping out where there is no place to step, yet you find yourself standing. Faith is reaching forth with empty hands, yet you find yourself coming back with a handful. Before we move any further, I want to give you my interpretation of **Hebrews 11:1**. This is not a new translation (we don't need any more of those), this is simply an interpretation.

"Now faith is the substance (conviction) of things hoped for, the evidence (reality) of things not seen." True, genuine, Bible-believing, Holy Ghost faith will cause you to see the unseen realities of the things of God, and put such a conviction, determination, purpose, desire, unstoppable resolve in your soul that you will pursue God with all that is within you. The attitude of your faith will give you the ability to transcend and look far beyond the physical, natural, temporal, and circumstantial realms in which you live every day in this world, beyond the plight of your own physical and emotional sufferings. You should be like the Canaanite woman mentioned in the former chapter, whose focus would not be derailed or knocked off balance by any critical or negative persuasion from our Lord's unbelieving disciples, nor by the physical maladies which attacked her daughter as a result of demon possession and oppression, nor was she slowed down by emotional maladies which would try to keep her from pursuing God. Her mentality and attitude was that of **Hebrews 12:2**: *"Looking unto Jesus the author and finisher of our faith; who for the joy that was set before him endured the cross, despising the shame, and is set down on the right hand of the throne of God."* This

54

attitude of faith motivates, encourages, and influences us to strive towards Him with ever abounding and immovable passion. The psalmist put it this way, *"My heart is fixed, O God, my heart is fixed..."* (Psalms 57:7) *"As the hart panteth after the water brooks, so panteth my soul after thee, O God. My soul thirsteth for God, for the living God: when shall I come and appear before God?"* (Psalms 42:1-2) *"But without faith it is impossible to please Him, for he that cometh to God, must believe that he is, and that he is a rewarder of them that diligently seek him."* (Hebrews 11:6) It would be easier to throw a rock from earth to the moon, than to try to please God not having faith. It would be easier to eat spoiled meat, than to try to please God and not have faith.

Our exercised faith activates and causes God to reciprocate His power and grace into our lives, and the natural byproduct of this process will please and glorify Him. Listed in Hebrews Chapter 11 are 20 examples of faith, the majority of which relate to extreme suffering. This shows us that faith is the most necessary ingredient in the elixir of suffering. This ingredient is the sweetener, if you will, and helps to remove the bitter taste of suffering which would try to completely overwhelm and consume the suffering saint.

The second word we must now define is **HOPE**. We gave this definition earlier, but it bears repeating. Hope is the belief that the outcome of our circumstances will yield rewards far greater than the pain endured. Faith and hope are coupled together. You cannot have the one without the other. Hope is knowing that at the end of the conflict, there is victory, rest, and reward **(Matthew 25:21-23; 1 Corinthians 3:11-15; Hebrews 11:6).** The offspring of hope is the assurance and confidence of God, because our hope is in the Lord. *"And of the work of righteousness shall be peace; and the effect and of righteousness quietness and assurance forever."* **(Isaiah 32:17)** With our eyes we see the waves and the wind, but with our faith and hope we see the wonderful Counselor. With our eyes we see the vicious storm which surrounds us, but with faith and hope we see our sovereign God which is our strength. With our eyes we see the flood of despair, but with our faith and hope we see the rainbow of God's deliverance.

I have never seen the attitude of faith more revealed than in a beautiful saint of God whose name was Carla. Carla was a devoted wife and a wonderful mother of three children. In the prime of her life she was stricken with a fatal terminal disease. Based on the condition of her illness, her exodus from this world was imminent. This is what she faced day to day. I don't know if I will be able to put into words what I actually saw in this great woman. This dear lady's life was consumed with treatments, doctor appointments, and medicine. Her joy and love of life, along with her deep faith in her Lord, caused everyone she knew, or who was exposed to her, to stand in amazement and astonishment by what they witnessed.

This woman was far happier and more content and satisfied than those who were wealthy, healthy, and without conflict in their lives. I will never forget the time when I ran into Carla in my missionary travels. We were coming out of a restaurant in northern Michigan and walking through the parking lot on a cold winter day. From a distance, running across that parking lot and toward me, was a tall slender woman waving her hands at me to get my attention. As she approached, getting closer and closer, I realized it was Carla. With a smile as bright and radiant as a morning sunrise, and with wide open arms she hugged me and said, "It's so good to see you brother." She then turned around and pointed at the building from which she'd come, and said, "I just finished one of my treatments." She went on to say, "The doctors have told me I don't have very long to live." There was not a hint of sadness or despair in her voice. In fact, I heard just the opposite. With great joy and happiness she declared, "I am so looking forward to seeing my Lord and Savior. I can't wait!" She talked to me with such great excitement, the same excitement as if she were explaining to me the pleasure of watching her child perform in a school play. Instead of you comforting Carla, it was Carla comforting you. You didn't need to encourage Carla to allow the peace of God to take over her life. She would explain to you how God had enveloped her life with His supernatural peace and presence. She was a beacon of the manifold grace of God. She ministered to her family and those around her, using her illness as an impetus to describe the intimate workings of the beauty, greatness and power of God! Everything that people would do to support, comfort, strengthen and help those in need, Carla, who was in the greatest of need, would do for others. She understood faith and hope and allowed God to take her to a sphere, plane, and dimension only she could experience and yet, she so desperately tried to explain it to others. Carla finally went home to be with the Lord. This wonderful servant of God, who labored so incessantly for His honor and glory in this life, won every battle and conquered every foe.

She knew the meaning of the apostle Paul, when he said, *"But we all, with open face beholding as in a glass the glory of the Lord, are changed into the same image from glory to glory, even as by the spirit of the Lord."* **(2 Corinthians 3:18)** In my 33 years of ministering the Word of God, I have never seen in the modern-day church, a woman like Carla.

CHAPTER 8

The secret of suffering is found in

THE ACTION OF FAITH

When faith moves, God responds, or we could say that God is moved by our faith. The Bible makes it so clear that we must live, move and walk by faith. In the Scriptures we are admonished to:

- Walk by faith **(2 Corinthians 5:7)**.
- Abound in faith **(2 Corinthians 8:7)**.
- Be strong in the faith **(Romans 4:20)**.
- Purify our hearts by faith **(Acts 15:9)**.
- Live by faith **(Romans 1:17)**.
- Stand in the faith **(2 Corinthians 1:24)**.
- Stand fast in the faith **(1 Corinthians 16:13)**.
- Build our faith in the Word of God **(Romans 10:17)**.
- Understand that our faith is most holy **(Jude 20)**.

Chapter 11 in Hebrews shows us the action of faith. In verse four, by faith Abel offered unto God a more excellent sacrifice than Cain. In verse five, by faith Enoch walked with God. In verse seven, by faith Noah, moved in fear, prepared an ark. In verse eight, by faith Abraham believed God. In verse eleven, by faith Sarah received strength to conceive.

In verses twenty through twenty-two, by faith Isaac blessed, Jacob worshiped, and Joseph gave commandment concerning his bones. In verses twenty-three through twenty-nine, by faith Moses refused to be called the son of Pharaoh's daughter. He chose rather to suffer affliction with the people of God than to enjoy the pleasures of sin for a season. By faith he esteemed the reproach of Christ greater riches than the treasures in Egypt. By faith he forsook Egypt, not fearing the wrath of the King, for he endured, as seeing HIM who is invisible. Through faith he kept The Passover and the sprinkling of the blood of the Lamb. By faith he and the nation of Israel passed through the Red Sea, and God gave to them a great victory. In verse thirty, by faith the walls of Jericho were brought down. In verse thirty-one, by faith Rahab the harlot was saved from death.

When we put our faith into action, God can and will do incredible things for us. In all of these cases of faith mentioned, there was suffering involved. Some of these saints of old experienced great physical suffering, some great emotional suffering, and several on this list endured both. The common denominator for all of these people who made it into "God's Hall of Faith" is that they were all victorious. They were all blessed of God. They all experienced our Lord in a wonderful and unique way. Your trial of affliction is a battle, struggle, and challenge, but God, through the action of your faith, will reveal to you that He is bigger than any circumstance in your life.

The action of faith invokes the ability of God. When David chose to go into the valley of Elah to do battle with the giant, Goliath, God met him there and gave him victory (1 Sam 17). David faced giant-like conflicts and heartbreaks all of his life. By faith he overcame King Saul who tried to kill him. By faith he overcame his rebellious son, Absalom, who tried to kill him. By faith he overcame enemy nations who tried to kill him. Like Job, David knew suffering.

At this point, you might confess that the action of faith cannot be embraced because of the weakness and frailty of your own personal faith. There is a great truth God would have us to know. If we put our weak, frail, little, and puny faith into the person and object of Jesus Christ, the son of

God, we can all become a people of great faith. The Gospels of Matthew, Mark, and Luke give us a great illustration of this truth. In **Matthew 8, Mark 4**, and in **Luke 8**, the story is told of Jesus, being in a boat with His disciples in the middle of the sea. He was so tired that He had fallen asleep. A great storm had arisen that caused the raging waves of waters to violently smash against their little vessel, tossing it to and fro in the darkness of the deep. The disciples were terrified! In a state of great fear and panic they implored their Lord with loud lamentations to, "…save us: we perish." **(Matthew 8:25)** In the midst of the tempest, the disciples didn't think they were going to make it out alive. When Jesus awoke, He sat there in the boat, looked at His disciples and chided them by saying, "…Why are ye fearful, O ye of little faith?" **(Matthew 8:26)** Mark's narration put it this way: "… How is it that ye have no faith?" **(Mark 4:40)**

The Spirit of God gave the historian, Luke, the following revelation concerning what Jesus had spoken during the incident: "… where is your faith?" **(Luke 8:25)** In these parallel passages it seems on the surface that there is a contradiction of statements from our Lord. Which statement did Jesus actually make? When you put all three narrations together, it's easy to come to the conclusion that Jesus made all three statements to His disciples simultaneously. The Holy Spirit, in these three Gospels, put them in perfect order to show a beautiful harmony of the Scriptures. When you put all three statements together you have a complete dialogue.

The problem was not that the disciples had little faith. The problem was that their little faith was not placed into the person and object of Jesus Christ, the Son of God. So, it was as if they had no faith. Therefore, Jesus naturally finishes His inquiry by saying "… Where is your faith..?" Let me give you an overview of this concept. The disciples' little faith was not in the person and object of Jesus Christ, the Son of God **(Matthew 8:26),** so it was as if they had no faith **(Mark 4:40);** therefore, Jesus naturally asked the question, "Where is your faith?" **(Luke 8:25)**

What a powerful question: "Where is your faith?" Our faith should not be in man, government, or any material resource. The believer's faith, in times of trouble or ease, must rest in the person of Christ alone! When Jesus spoke the words "… If ye have faith as a grain of mustard seed, ye shall say unto this mountain, remove hence to yonder place; and it shall remove; and nothing shall be impossible unto you." **(Matthew 17:20)** When little, weak, frail, puny, and small faith is placed into the proper object, the person of Christ, Almighty God, that faith, being as small as a grain of mustard seed, can become mountain moving faith. What type of suffering has produced a mountain in your life? Sickness, emotional malady, tragedy, fear, addiction? Your body and mind may be weak and suffering. You may feel that your faith is weak too. But, if the whole concentration and focus of your weak faith is placed on Christ, then the action and motion of your faith will be great and God will move.

CHAPTER 9

The secret *of suffering is found in*

THE PERSON AND
SECRET PLACE OF PRAYER

"In my distress I call upon the Lord, and cried unto my God: he heard my voice out of his temple, and my cry came before him, even into his ears."

(PSALMS 18:6)

The greatest support, ability and opportunity in a severe time of suffering is Christ, our Advocate. Our prayer and faith, or should I say our prayer of faith, directly and intimately connects us to the sufficiency and help that is secured for us in our Lord. God talks to us through His Word and we talk to God through prayer.

Prayer is not a religious observance. It is an outgrowth and an expression of one who is in an intimate relationship. Prayer is not ceremonial. It is communication which results in communion and closeness. Prayer is not a series of chants, a diatribe, or a scripted dialogue to be outwardly performed as an Orthodox ritual so that others can see **(Matthew 6:5, 7)**. Prayer is a conversation between you and God, as one who is talking to a close friend or someone who is deeply loved.

Imagine for a moment. If you did not speak to your best friend for a long period of time, your friend would probably begin to feel neglected or avoided. That friend may wonder if you just didn't care anymore about the relationship. It would be hard to maintain a close, intimate friendship with someone with whom you hardly communicate.

God desires us to communicate with Him concerning every area of our life. We can talk to Him about the little matters, as well as the big matters. Remember, He's our Heavenly Father, and as a father He wants to be involved in every aspect and area of our life, especially when we suffer. When we are suffering, God wants us to draw close to Him...I mean run to Him. He wants us to share and express every feeling and emotion: fear, anxiety, frustration, stress, anger, bewilderment, bitterness, and questioning. God wants it all and He can handle it all. When you read the expressions and utterances of Job, in his suffering, he exclaimed all of these emotions.

When we are suffering and we pray, we experience fellowship and communion with God **(Psalms 5:3)**, the supernatural presence of God **(Psalms 27:4; 42:1-2)**, a peace that passeth all understanding **(Philippians 4:6-7)**, and the help we need with our every care **(1 Peter 5:7; Romans 8:26; Hebrews 4:16)**.

What is prayer? Prayer is simply asking. If we are not praying, we are not asking; if we are not asking, we are not praying. In **James 4:4,** we are told, *"...ye have not because ye ask not."* Another element of prayer is praise, thanksgiving, and worship. This form of prayer is not a request, but instead, reciprocating to God our love and appreciation for what He has done.

The Person of Prayer

The object of our prayer is not an idol of wood, stone, or some religious symbol. The object of our prayer is the person of Christ. Think about this for a moment, beloved. When we look to God in time of suffering and call out and cry out to Him, we are entering into the very throne room of the Alpha and Omega, the beginning and the ending, the first and the last, the preexisting and self-existing God, the God who is in need of nothing, the author, sustainer, and finisher of all things, the source, support, and end of all things, the great I AM. In prayer, you are talking to Jesus, the lover of your soul.

The following people are biblical examples of what it means to diligently seek and pursue Christ as the object and focus of prayer in time of suffering.

When the disciples were filled with fear in the middle of a fierce storm, they immediately sought the Lord for help, "And, behold, there arose a great tempest in the sea, insomuch that the ship was covered with the waves: but he was asleep. And his disciples came to him, and awoke him, saying [prayed], Lord save us: we perish." **(Matthew 8:24-25)**

Jairus, a broken-hearted father who came to Jesus, expressed his heart by asking the Lord to come and help his daughter: "...And he fell down at Jesus' feet, and besought [prayed], him that he would come into his house." **(Luke 8:41)**

A woman who was very ill with a sickness for 12 years, brought the burden of her physical pain to the Lord. By faith she reached out "...And touched the border of his garment"... "Declared [prayed] unto him" **(Luke 8:44, 47)** that it was she who had, in faith, pursued, believed, and was healed as a result.

Martha and Mary, the sisters of Lazarus, brought their anger, sorrow, faith and disappointment to the Lord. Listen to their words: "Then said [prayed] Martha unto Jesus, Lord, if thou hadst been here, my brother had not died. But I know, that even now, whatsoever thou wilt ask of God, God will give it thee." **(John 11:21,32)** They unloaded a world of emotion on our Lord.

Stephen, in his dying moment, as he was being stoned for his faith and devoted service for Christ, looked up into heaven and called upon God. *"And they stoned Stephen, calling upon God, and saying [praying], Lord Jesus, receive my spirit."* **(Acts 7:59)** Jesus must be the only object and focus of our praying.

The Place of Prayer

The place of prayer means that we should be in a constant and continual state of praying. From the sanctuary of our soul, we can at all times cry out to God. In our sufferings and afflictions, our place of prayer should be without ceasing **(1 Thessalonians 5:17)**. King David said it this way, *"What time I am afraid, I will trust in thee."* **(Psalms 56:3)** When Jesus preached His great "Sermon on the Mount," He promised those who would pray that God sees the praying saint and He will reward the praying saint, *"But thou, when thou prayest, enter into thy closet and when thou hast shut the door, pray to thy Father which seeth in secret; and thy Father which seeth in secret shall reward thee openly."* **(Matthew 6:6)**

I recall the times in my own agony, when my son was sick and suffering, the fear and uncertainty I would often feel. In that very low and dark time of my life, I recall finding that private place where I could be alone with God and just pray. I would go down upon my face in defeat and anguish, but every time God would somehow and in a very unique way touch and strengthen me. I did not receive from the Lord in that prayer closet the assurance that my desired outcome of the conflict would come to pass, but rather, He gave me the peace, comfort, and knowledge that He was with me. In that moment, it was all I needed.

Jesus was the perfect example of finding that alone intimate place with the Heavenly Father to share His burdens, so that he could receive strength. After Jesus heard of the death and unlawful murder of His friend and cousin the great John the Baptist, He tried to find refuge in a desert place. When He had arrived in that desert place, He found that the multitudes had followed Him. Jesus, being moved with compassion, spent the entire day healing and ministering to the masses.

After the long hard day of ministry work, Jesus then commanded the multitude to sit down on the grass and performed the mighty miracle of feeding over 5,000 people with only five loaves and two fishes. During all of these series of events, Jesus, no doubt, was grieving and filled with sorrow over the martyrdom of the beloved John the Baptist. Finally, Jesus sent the multitudes away and commanded His disciples to get into a ship. He instructed them to go over to the other side and eventually He would meet them. Then we find Jesus going into the mountain, apart from everyone, to pray. He needed sustaining grace, comfort, strength, and rest.

All of which He obtained, as He met His Heavenly Father alone in that quiet mountain place. *"And when he had sent the multitudes away, he went up into a mountain apart to pray: and when the evening was come, he was there alone."* (Matthew 14:23)

Even when our Lord was in the midst of His disciples, they would often find Him alone praying: *"And it came to pass, as he was alone praying, his disciples were with him..."* (Luke 9:18)

Again we find Jesus alone in a mountain praying all night: *"And it came to pass in those days, that he went out into a mountain to pray, and continued all night in prayer to God."* (Luke 6:12). This is interesting. After Jesus prayed all night, He then went and called His twelve disciples, healed the multitudes, cast out devils, and preached a powerful sermon. Our Lord would always, before or during a trial of affliction, anchor and gird Himself in prayer. The example the Lord set for His disciples would be a constant reminder to them of what they must do in times of great conflict.

The beautiful glorious truth is God is always available and at any time He will hear the cries, burdens, fears, sorrows, and desires of our heart, *"Evening, and morning, and at noon, will I pray, and cry aloud: and he shall hear my voice."* (Psalms 55:18)

When we pray, we literally enter into the throne room of God (Hebrew 4:15-16). We can by faith find warmth and comfort by reclining in the bosom of our Savior and by whispering into His ear (John 13:23-25). Prayer touches and moves the very heart of our Lord (Luke 8:44-48; Matthew 15:22-28). In the following passage notice how far, deep, and close we can burrow and nestle into the presence of God:

"He that dwelleth in the secret place of the Most High shall abide under the shadow of the Almighty. I will say of the Lord, he is my refuge and my fortress: my God; in him will I

trust. Surely he shall deliver thee from the snare of the fowler, and from the noisome pestilence. He shall cover thee with his feathers, and under his wings shalt thou trust: his truth shall be thy shield and buckler. Thou shalt not be afraid for the terror by night; nor for the arrow that flies by day; nor for the pestilence that walketh in darkness; nor for the destruction that wasteth at noonday."

(Psalms 91:1-6)

This secret place is a place that must be sought by all those who suffer. Jesus knew this secret place and would often go there. In this secret place, there is a rare and calming revelation and communion with the Most High. In this realm and sphere there is a supernatural confidence and an inner knowing which causes the soul to be still. Though the tumultuous storm may rage from without and the fierce heat of trials may beat against our clay tabernacles, we can find shelter beneath the protection of His wings, tucked away within the embrace of His feathers. Here no disease, fear, worry, terror or adversarial conflict can touch us, whether it be physical or emotional maladies, financial or relational challenges or spiritual failures resulting from a moral collapse. The feathers of His wings, which cover us, form an impenetrable shield and buckler that can never be compromised nor breached, neither by day or night. The wings and feathers of our Savior shows us the "brooding-over" of His "motherly love," providing 24-hour-a-day surveillance and watchful care for His children. Why stand we in the outer court, when we can enter into the Holy of Holies, the inner sanctuary, where the appearance of His glory can be seen and experienced?

We must dwell and abide there continually, for only then will we know the secret and the sacred fulfillment of God moving upon our heart and mind with His ministry of comfort. Often suffering is the impetus and motivation which sustains our continual appearance before the presence of God. Once you put yourself there and stay, you will never want to leave. Why? Because you will experience the beauty of the Lord, and a foretaste of heaven on earth of which nothing in this life can compare. The psalmist

David put it this way: *"One thing have I desired of the Lord, that will I seek after; that I may dwell in the house of the Lord all the days of my life, to behold the beauty of the Lord, and to inquire in his Temple."* (Psalms 27:4)

This incredible truth of dwelling in the secret place of the Most High and abiding under the shadow of the Almighty is beautifully illustrated in the following verses and comments:

- *"Let him kiss me with the kisses of his mouth: for thy love is better than wine."* (Song of Solomon 1:2)
- *"Kiss the son, lest he be angry, and ye perish from the way, when his wrath is kindled but a little. Blessed are all they that put their trust in him."* (Psalms 2:12)

The Song of Solomon 1:2, along with **Psalms 2:12**, portrays in a beautiful metaphor the intimate desire and love that God has for His covenant people: Israel, the church (which is the body of Christ), and the individual believer. Just as the physical senses are awakened and quickened in a relationship that is pure and right, so also are the spiritual senses awakened and quickened as intimate fellowship and communion is diligently sought and maintained with our Lord **(Hebrews 11:6)**.

In **Psalms 2:12** we are admonished to *"kiss the son, lest he be angry, and ye perish from the way, when his wrath is kindled but a little. Blessed are all they that put their trust in him." "Kiss the son..."* is the Old Testament way of saying, *"Believe on the Lord Jesus Christ, and thou shalt be saved."* **(Acts 16:31)** *"Kiss the son..."* goes far beyond initial belief and trust in Christ for salvation. This is a term of endearment, intimacy, affinity, and deep affection! Our God is personal, not aloof, detached, or unconcerned. He is called our "Heavenly Father" and He loves to give good things to His children **(Luke 11:13)**, to *"freely give us all things."* **(Romans 8:32)** He knows all of your needs and will supply them **(Matthew 6:32)**. God is so concerned, so connected, so involved that He even knows the very number of hairs on your head **(Matthew 10:30)**. The only way to know such intimate information about another is to be close to that person. Our God is close, *"a God at hand... and not a God afar off"* (Jeremiah 23:23). He is a God that will touch you (Matthew 8:2; John 9:6), hold you in His bosom (John 13:23, 25), caress you with His hands as He washes your feet (John 13:4-13), enclose you in the palm of His hand (John 10:27-30), cook a meal for you (John 21:9-12), call you by name (John 20:16; 21:15, 17), listen and respond to your concerns, fears, doubts, and weaknesses (Jeremiah 33:3; Matthew 11:2-6), and comfort and care for you (John 14:26-27; 1 Peter 5:7). Well Glory!!! God never moves away from us, but we move away from Him in thought, words or actions. God wants us to kiss Him (Psalms 2:12a).

Kiss God in faithful devotion

There are different kinds of kisses. All kisses (save the kiss of lust) say, "I love you!" Some kisses say, "You're my friend. You're precious to me!" Abraham was called the friend of God (James 2:23). Friends talk to one another, care for one another, give to one another, respect one another, will never abandon or betray one another. Are you a friend to God?

Kiss God in fervent desire

The spiritual bedroom of love and intimacy, which can only be found as we dwell and abide with Him in that secret place, goes far beyond the physical bedroom of love and intimacy experienced by a husband and wife bound together for life through holy matrimony. Knowing God through our spiritual senses greatly supersedes any physical experience in this life, whether it be in time of good or in time of infliction as a result of suffering. Solomon uses the physical realm to parallel the spiritual realm having to do with our relationship, fellowship, and sweet communion with God. The love of His life brings out, for us, the essence of what God desires and wants for all of His people to experience in Him. Some kisses are passionate, and filled with the fervency to be as close and as intimate as possible.

To feel warmth, breath, the sensation of oneness: skin touching skin, mind touching mind, heart touching heart, and soul touching soul!

Other writers of the Bible also describe this type of affection when communing with God. "And thou shalt love the LORD thy God with all thy heart, and with all thy soul, and with all thy might" **(Deuteronomy 6:5)**; "I will love thee, O LORD my strength" **(Psalms 18:1)**; "As the hart panteth after the water brooks, so panteth my soul after thee, O God. My soul thirsteth for God, for the living God: when shall I come and appear before God" **(Psalms 42:1-2)**; "My heart is fixed, O God, my heart is fixed…" **(Psalms 57:7)**; "My soul followeth hard after thee…" **(Psalms 63:8)**; "That I may know him, and the power of his resurrection, and the fellowship of his sufferings, being made conformable unto his death" **(Philippians 3:10)**; "Yea doubtless, and I count all things but loss for the excellency of the knowledge of Christ Jesus my Lord: for whom I have suffered the loss of all things, and do count them but dung, that I may win Christ." **(Philippians 3:8)** Notice how suffering is directly linked to knowing Christ intimately, through diligent perusal of Him, only to be found and experienced as we dwell and abide with Him in that secret place.

Do you see in these above verses the passion, the desire, the determination, the yearning, the fervor, the commitment, the need, and the longing to be close to God? To commune with Him, to embrace Him? To burn for Him? To kiss Him?

Some kisses are out of control. Every sensation (sight, touch, smell, taste, and hearing) is the singular focus of the one reciprocating and benefiting from the passion and delivery of such affection. Such should be our love, fellowship, communion, worship, and energy toward God. We should love Him with all of our being, with every ounce of strength that our soul can supply and put out, with an earnestness that cannot be measured, with a length and depth that reaches into eternity. O that God would know this is how I love Him and want to love Him and long for Him!

The apostle Paul put it this way. *"For to me to live is Christ, and to die is gain."* **(Philippians 1:21)** Paul recognized this about Christ: *"…who loved me, and gave Himself for me."* **(Galatians 2:20)** "Kiss the son" is the desire of God for His people. No pleasure in this world can offer dignity and sublimity that compare to the kisses of the Son of God! *"Let him kiss me with the kisses of his mouth: For thy love is better than wine."* (Song of Solomon 1:2)

Kiss the face of Christ and forever thou shalt be one **(John 17:23)**.

Kiss the face of Christ and adore the greatness of The Son **(Psalms 4:4; 1 John 1:4-5)**.

Kiss the face of Christ, none will be like its embrace **(Psalms 34:8)**.

Kiss the face of Christ, for the provision of His grace **(2 Corinthians 12:9-10)**.

Kiss the face of Christ, none but Him can gratify.

Kiss the face of Christ, your soul shall satisfy **(John 4:14)**.

Kiss the face of Christ, your Bridegroom, champion, and King.

Kiss the face of Christ, and His canticles you will sing **(Revelation 2:22)**.

Kiss the face of Christ, thou art His joy and delight **(Psalms 16:3)**.

Kiss the face of Christ, for thou art precious in His sight **(Psalms 139:17)**.

Kiss the face of Christ, and thou shalt never fall **(2 Peter 1:5, 10)**.

Kiss the face of Christ, and enjoy your All in All **(1 Corinthians 15:28)**.

Kiss God in fellowship and delight

When you kiss God, you remain close and near to Him in that secret place. When a kiss is long in duration or often repeated, there are intimate details discovered and experienced, knowledge that can only be obtained because closeness has occurred. When something or someone is greatly loved and adored, the object of that affection cannot get enough. More and more is desired. Such is the case of having fellowship and communion with God. Peter was enjoying the glories of the transfiguration of Christ so much on the mount that he did not want to leave **(Matthew 17:1-8)**.

"Be thou my strong habitation, whereunto I may continually resort..."

(PSALMS 71:3)

"Nevertheless I am continually with thee: thou hast holden me by my right hand."

(PSALMS 73:23)

When you enter into that secret place and kiss the Savior, and the Savior kisses you, the world with its calls, cares, sorrows, burdens, stresses, conflicts, infirmities, and sufferings will all become dull and eventually fade into nothing! The lovers of the world that would entice, ensnare, and entrap your soul will have nothing to offer **(1 John 2:15)**. For the bitter wine of this world, in whatever form it comes, has no comparison to the sweet wine of the Kisses of God, which can only be found in that secret place!

CHAPTER 10

The secret of suffering is found in

THE PASSION OF PRAYER

There are two words that describe the very nature and essence of prayer. These words are "intercession" and "supplication."

Intercession: a going out from ourselves to seek the care of others.

Supplication: the very soul of prayer: one thing is greatly needed, and that need is intensely felt and earnestly sought after through much pleading and perseverance before God.

"The Lord hath heard my supplication; the Lord will receive my prayer."

(PSALMS 6:9)

One of the greatest examples of intercession and supplication found in the Bible is the story of Abraham entreating the Lord for his nephew, Lot. God revealed to Abraham that He was going to judge and destroy the cities of Sodom and Gomorrah. This is a beautiful picture of the prayer of supplication.

In this story we see Abraham's love, care, and devotion for his family.

Abraham pleaded with God not to destroy the cities, because he did not want Lot and his family to be killed as a result of God's judgment against the wickedness of that place. The actual prayer is found in **Genesis 18:22-33**. In verses 22 and 23 we find the real essence, foundation, and spiritual work of prayer: "But Abraham stood yet before the LORD, and Abraham drew near, and said, 'Wilt thou also destroy the righteous with the wicked?'"

Notice the position of prayer. Abraham was standing between God and the cities, and simply having a conversation with the Lord. His conversation was passionate, filled with burden and heartfelt emotion. Also, we see that Abraham "drew near." He got close to God, as close as he could. I believe with all of my heart that the patriarch, Abraham, was standing right next to God, face to face.

The word picture I have in my mind of this event would be equivalent to a major league manager coming out of the dugout to discuss a call with the umpire. If you notice, most of those discussions are quite intense, as the umpire and the manager are almost nose-to-nose. Or I think of it as a little child getting as close as possible to Mom or Dad, to ask for that one thing, which is greatly needed or desired.

Abraham starts his prayer by saying, "Peradventure (what if, suppose) there be fifty righteous within the city: wilt Thou also destroy and not spare the place for the fifty righteous that are therein?" Abraham starts his plea to God by using the number fifty. Then as you read, he moves from fifty to forty-five, then to forty. As he continued to persevere and make his requests known unto God, he went down to thirty, then twenty, and finally, ten. Abraham, while praying, made an appeal to the righteousness and holiness of God (verse 25), "Shall not the Judge of all the earth do right?" The attitude of Abraham's prayer was filled with humility (verse 27): "Now, I have taken upon me to speak unto the LORD, which am but dust and ashes..." Abraham was so earnest, diligent, and unrelenting in his pursuit to get God's attention in this matter that he feared the Lord may be losing patience with him (verse 30), "Oh let not the LORD be angry, and I will speak..."

As you read this passage of Scripture, you will notice by the end of the prayer, there was a huge change of emotion on Abraham's part. He just got to the place where passion, from a broken heart, superseded (replaced) everything else in his consciousness. The plea is now raw, forceful, and monosyllabic, fixed and focused with the intensity of his request (verse 31): "Behold now, I have taken upon me to speak unto the LORD..." Just before Abraham ended his prayer, his progression seems to crescendo into a final lamentation and cry for help (verse 32): "I will speak yet but this once…"

The Lord heard and answered Abraham's prayer. During this whole time of prayer, God and Abraham experienced sweet fellowship and communion with one another. Often, this is what intercession and supplication will produce.

Passionate praying means we never give up on what we are seeking from God. Jesus said, *"Men ought always to pray and not to faint."* **(Luke 18:1)** *But if from thence thou shalt seek the LORD thy God, thou shalt find [cause Him to hear and respond] Him, if thou seek Him with all thy heart and with all thy soul."* **(Deuteronomy 4:29)**

Those who are physically suffering and desiring healing from the Lord should not give up in their request for such a blessing. One must also be sensitive enough before the Lord to seek His wisdom and direction for the manner in which to pray. I recall distinctly when my wife was pregnant with our son, Tiger B, I would often pray that everything would be fine and there be no complications. I would also pray that God would protect my wife and baby, and allow for a safe delivery and a normal healthy child.

One night while working out at the gym, I was praying...then all of a sudden, a prompting, a stirring, moved in my soul. The unction was very clear. His voice spoke so loud to me, and His message was unmistakable. The Holy Spirit said to me, *"Do not pray this anymore. Just know that I am in control."*

I changed my prayer: "Lord not my will, but thy will be done."

The following verses will show the manner in which we must passionately, diligently, repentantly, and humbly seek the Lord in prayer:

"But if from thence thou shalt seek the Lord thy God, thou shalt find him, if thou seek him with all thy heart and with all thy soul."

(DEUTERONOMY 4:29)

"If my people, which are called by my name, shall humble themselves, and pray, and seek my face, and turn from their wicked ways; then will I hear from heaven, and will forgive their sin, and will heal their land."

(2 CHRONICLES 7:14)

As we pursue God through prayer, there are three things that He requires us to do, so we can receive from Him, find His answers, and walk through the door of His will: *"Ask, and it shall be given you; seek, and ye shall find; knock, and it shall be opened unto you: for everyone that asketh receiveth; and he that seeketh findeth; and to him that knocketh it shall be opened."* **(Matthew 7:7-8)**

There are other attitudes of prayer we must observe so we can find favor with God and receive from Him those things that we seek and greatly need in our lives. The favor of God is available to any child of God who would diligently pursue and seek after the heart, mind, desire, purpose, plan and will of the Lord **(Ephesians 5:16; Hebrews 11:6)**. God Himself said of David, *"...I have found David the son of Jesse, a man after mine own heart which shall fulfill all My will..."* **(Acts 13:21)**

King David is the greatest picture and portrait of Christ found in the Scriptures. Yet this great king had several problems, conflicts, and complexities in his life. King David knew heartbreak and failure. David committed adultery and murder, he had a bad temper, at times he lied and was rebellious against God, yet through all those failures and dark clouds, he had a heart, passion and love for God which was unparalleled. Many times in the Psalms, David expresses and avows his great love for his Lord **(Psalms 18:1; 116:1)**. In this we can take comfort, because even though we fail and have brokenness and deep emotional scars and wounds, the Holy Spirit of

God, in His omniscience (God knows all things) can pierce through the maze of our failures, shortcomings and hurts, and see that we love and desire Him most of all. The greatest way to express this towards our Savior is to passionately pursue Him in prayer. Keep asking! Keep seeking! Keep knocking!

Passionate praying means we pray in faith. We pray believing. As we approach God, we do so with earnest confidence and expectation. This keeps hope alive and burning within our soul. This type of praying yields blessed assurance: "And all things, whatsoever ye shall ask in prayer, believing, ye shall receive." **(Matthew 21:22)**

"But let him ask in faith, nothing wavering. For he that wavereth is like a wave of the sea driven with the wind and tossed."

(JAMES 1:6)

"And this is the confidence that we have in him, that, if we ask any thing according to his will, he heareth us."

(1 JOHN 5:14)

"Let us draw near with a true heart in full assurance of faith..."

(HEBREWS 10:22)

"I will therefore that men pray every where, lifting up holy hands, without wrath and doubting."

(1 TIMOTHY 2:8)

There is an interesting element of prayer mentioned in **1 Timothy 2:8**. We should not harbor wrath or bitterness in our hearts towards others as we make our supplication before the Lord. Bitterness only eats at its own hurts. Bitterness will affect and distract our praying. Often, when we suffer, it is a time that God can bring great cleansing into our life, especially from the defilement of bitterness which can so easily cloud our soul. When you are willing to forgive others, it is then you become most "Christ-like."

"Night and day praying exceedingly ..."

(1 THESSALONIANS 3:10)

This describes extreme praying...a fierce and desperate approach in our praying. This is praying with a resolve and steadfastness which cannot be derailed!

CHAPTER 11

The secret of suffering is found in

THE PERSEVERANCE OF PRAYER

The passion of prayer is closely related to another crucial ingredient in the elixir of prayer. This very important ingredient is perseverance. Without perseverance in prayer we are bound to always fail in all matters of our faith and walk with God.

Every failure in the Christian life is a result of our failure to pray. Daily prayer is as important as daily drinking water or eating food. Just as food and water sustain physical life, daily prayer sustains spiritual life. Without the physical necessities of food and water, one would grow weaker and weaker day by day, finally becoming unconscious. The same is true of the spiritual realm; without the daily diet of the Word of God and prayer, our spiritual life would gradually weaken, and finally, the believer would experience a spiritual deadness. Not a spiritual death resulting in the loss of salvation, but a spiritual death resulting in the loss of power, the presence of God, and the bearing of fruit in the Christian life.

"For to be carnally minded [embracing the physical, natural, temporal, self-gratifying, sinful realm of life] is death; but to

be spiritually minded [embracing the Godly, biblical, super-
natural, eternal realm] is life and peace."

(ROMANS 8:6)

The story of Jesus praying in the garden prior to His arrest and crucifixion is the perfect example of perseverance in prayer. In **Matthew 26:37-46**,
Peter, James, and John were privileged to be with our Lord in the garden
of Gethsemane as He prayed to the Heavenly Father about His fears, the
impending doom of the crucifixion, and all the degradations of the cross
that would shortly befall Him.

While in the garden, Jesus asked His disciples to: *"Watch and pray,*
that ye enter not into temptation...and... tarry ye here and watch with
me." **(Matthew 26:37, 41)** He would leave them for a time and go deeper
into the garden and pray alone before His Heavenly Father. Jesus in His
humanity needed prayer support, and asked His most trusted disciples to be
diligent, alert, on guard, and to labor with Him before the Heavenly Father
in prayer. Our Lord was filled with sorrow and even felt like He would experience an untimely death because of the emotional pain, pressure, and stress
He felt and experienced in that garden.

After about an hour, Jesus returned to His disciples only to find them
sleeping. They failed to persevere in their praying. And Jesus said to them,
"...What, could ye not watch with Me one hour?" **(Matthew 26:40)** Jesus
went back into His place of prayer within the garden a second time and
asked His disciples again to continue to watch and pray with Him. Jesus'
praying was so intense in the garden that He "...sweat as it were great drops
of blood..." **(Luke 22:44)**

When He returned to His disciples after being in prayer (the amount of
time He spent in prayer is not disclosed in Scripture), He again found them
sleeping **(Matthew 26:43)**. He departed a third time to continue praying. At
this point it would behoove us to take a close look at Jesus' actual prayer in
the garden. He prayed, "O My Father, if it be possible let this cup pass from
Me; nevertheless not as I will but as Thy wilt... O My Father, if this cup
may not pass away from Me, accept I drink it, thy will be done." **(Matthew**

82

26:39, 42) In the parallel passage of **Luke 22:42**, it is stated that Jesus said, "Nevertheless not My will but Thine be done." The magnificence of this prayer is that so many of our own human frailties, weaknesses, sufferings, and fears can be seen in the humanity of Christ. He approached the Heavenly Father in complete submission, humble and willing to perform God's will despite His own human fears and desires. This glimpse into the real manhood of Christ should comfort, encourage, and motivate every believer concerning the act and necessity of prayer.

Hebrews 5:7 is revealing, giving us a commentary and explanation of our Lord's very real human experience in that garden: "Who in the days of his flesh, when he had offered up prayers and supplications with strong crying and tears unto him that was able to save him from death, and was heard in that he feared."

Please notice the emotions of strong crying, tears, and fear. In your life right now, are you feeling this way? The intimacy and earnestness with which He prayed is so expressive that He, like a little child frightened and scared of the unknown, referred to His Heavenly Father as "Abba," which means "Daddy" **(Mark 14:36)**. The word picture and metaphor is very powerful here. I can only relate it to my own children. At times when they were little, if they experienced fear, they would clutch my hand or motion to be held by me for safety and protection. Jesus knew where to run; He knew where to go, to His Daddy, His Heavenly Father!

The great truth you must see here, is that Jesus spent much time in prayer. He did not give up, quit, falter, fail, cease or faint in prayer! In contrast, the disciples slumbered, fell asleep and slept in sorrow, failing to pray. They had sorrow because of fear and uncertainty; their Lord had many enemies, and they lived in a state of constant apprehension. The disciples had been tirelessly working and laboring with their Lord in ministry, which no doubt left them fatigued and exhausted.

Jesus' counsel to His disciples was to, "Watch and pray, that ye enter not into temptation." He went on to explain and teach, "...the spirit is indeed willing but the flesh is weak." Temptations come in various forms and in many different ways. There is the temptation of lust for self-gratification and pleasure, and then there are temptations which come in the form of trials to test our faith. Whatever your burden and suffering may be (sorrow, hurt, fear, worry, anxiety, confusion, frustration, anger, bitterness, resentment, addiction, lust, guilt, self-condemnation, or perhaps some physical infirmities or maladies) the answer, help, and healing can be found and experienced as we persevere before the great Psychologist and Physician of Heaven in the quiet, solitude garden of prayer.

I chose this particular event to show that even though our Lord knew the horrors that would soon befall Him, He received from His Heavenly Father the grace, strength, and ability to endure and fulfill the will of His God. He obtained strength and courage through prayer! This is the greatest example of perseverance in prayer which can be found in the Word of God.

There is another wonderful truth in this story I do not want you to miss. As Jesus was in the garden of Gethsemane praying, He desired that His disciples would watch and pray with Him. This is a beautiful illustration of our current position with Jesus as our great High Priest, actually praying with us in our time of need, making our requests known to the Heavenly Father, as we find ourselves in the garden experiencing fears as a result of our own sufferings.

"Seeing then that we have a great high priest, that is passed into the heavens, Jesus the son of God, let us hold fast our profession. For we have not an high priest which cannot be touched with the feelings of our infirmities; but was in all points tempted like as we are, yet without sin." **(Hebrews 4:14-15)** Our great High Priest, Jesus, is touched with every burden, hurt, sorrow, pain, affliction and emotion that you feel. The great truth of the garden of Gethsemane is this: when we pray, we are not only praying to our Lord, but with our Lord! And our Lord, at the same time, is praying not only with us, but for us! As we kneel and pray to our Lord, He is right there kneeling beside us, and with us, making our requests known to God. Jesus, on our behalf will go before the Heavenly Father and will articulate and express every infirmity, fear, and groaning of our suffering heart, *"Likewise the Spirit also helpeth our infirmities: for we know not what we should pray for as we ought: but the Spirit itself*

maketh intercession for us with groanings which cannot be uttered."
(Romans 8:26)

Think about it, beloved: every feeling of your emotions, and detail of your thoughts are heard, understood, and felt by the Lord Jesus, in the person of the Holy Spirit, and are taken before the Heavenly Father, clearly expressed as to the very thing you need because your Savior was praying with you. This is true intimacy with God, and the very thing which takes place when we passionately persevere in prayer. This type of praying touches and moves God. What we must learn from all of this is that no matter what happens to us in life, or whatever challenges we may face, we can endure, persevere, overcome, and obtain the victory over any circumstance or event, because we prevailed in prayer!

CHAPTER 12

The secret of suffering is found in

THE PROMISE OF PRAYER

As we passionately pray and persevere in prayer, God promises He will hear and answer our prayer. Prayer gives us the confidence that God is in control, and we can rest in that assurance.

"Call unto Me, and I will answer thee, and shew thee great and mighty things which thou knowest not."

(JEREMIAH 33:3)

The sweet "weeping-prophet" Jeremiah, has found himself in much tribulation. Tribulation as a result of doing God's will and obeying God's command. This steadfast prophet had a hard message to give and deliver — a message of God's judgment and impending doom, if the Lord's people failed to repent and return to their God.

Jeremiah had very few converts. His sermons were despised and rejected. Jeremiah knew suffering; his life and ministry was very, very, hard. Jeremiah was persecuted by his own family **(Jeremiah 12:5)**. The people in his own hometown came against him **(Jeremiah 11:21)**. He was hated and sorely persecuted by the religious system and leaders of his day.

The following is a resume of his extreme suffering and the rejection he endured from his own nation: he was arrested, beaten, whipped and put into stocks. Jeremiah's hands and legs were bound securing him locked in a contorted position. This was done so the body would produce severe cramping in the muscles **(Jeremiah 20:2)**. Jeremiah was almost killed by a wild mob of religionists after he preached one of his messages **(Jeremiah 26:7-9)**. He was also falsely accused of treason, and for this he was arrested, flogged, and cast into the palace prison.

One of the most horrific experiences of Jeremiah was forced upon him by the wicked King Zedekiah. At the command of this despot, Jeremiah, hung by his wrists, was lowered into a filthy, miry pit. The intent was Jeremiah would be down there long enough to possibly starve to death. After the king relented, he was rescued, but he had sunk deep into that filth, and it took thirty men to pull him out. One can only imagine the darkness, coldness, dampness, and foul odor of that awful place. I wanted you to get a clear understanding of Jeremiah's peril.

So now we come to the epic declaration given by God, Himself, in relation to the promise of prayer. It is important to note God gives this promise to Jeremiah in the midst of his extreme suffering. This proclamation of the Lord given to Jeremiah should serve as an example for all of us to follow and embrace as we endure suffering. This message of promise came to Jeremiah the second time that Jeremiah was shut up in the prison.

First, notice God's invitation: "call unto me..." To whom are we calling? The King! Our Heavenly Father! Our Savior! We cry out to the one who said "The very hairs of your head are all numbered." **(Matthew 10:30)** God knew where Jeremiah was, and He knows where you are. He asks us to make our appeal, to state our cause, to bear our heart, and communicate to Him our conflict. Our pleas and calling may be mixed with bitterness, anger, confusion, and much sorrow and grief. There is no condition attached to this invitation. There is no right way or wrong way to express our need. He just simply says, "call unto me..." What a wonderful invitation: to be summoned by the one who knows all things, by the one who has all power, to enter in before His Majesty and to take refuge within the Holy of Holies.

The psalmist cried out in time of much perplexity, *"No man cared for my soul..."* **(Psalms 142:4)** But God is just the opposite. He cares for your soul. The one who makes this open-armed appeal, who is so approachable, so accessible, and always ready to hear, is the same one who says in the New Testament, *"Come unto me, all ye that labor and are heavy laden, and I will give you rest. Take my yoke upon you, and learn of me: for I am meek and lowly in heart: and ye shall find rest unto your souls. For my yoke is easy, and my burden is light."* **(Matthew 11:28-30)**

Jesus cares for your soul. The soul is the tabernacle which houses all of our feelings and emotions. All of our fears, struggles, anguish, and perplexities are all anchored within the soul. This invitation that God gives to His bereaved prophet is the same invitation He gives to you. This is an invitation to rest, to have the burden lifted, and the yoke of our worries eased by the one who will take them from us and carry the load that is far too heavy to bear alone.

Even Jesus taught when our soul feels the weight of the burdensome yoke of bitter conflict, we will learn of Him. The glories and companionship of Christ will bring enlightenment, revelation, and understanding that far exceeds this tangible world, and will lighten our load because we will see things from God's perspective. This invitation of prayer bids us to walk through the heavenly door, as the Apostle John did in Revelation the fourth chapter, and view the heavenly scene, where the one who sits on the throne rules over all. He is adored and worshiped by the redeemed, because they have experienced victories in all the battles of life.

And now they're about to get a glimpse of the outcome of all things. The tragic fall in Genesis has come to a perfect end, where all "bad" is abolished, and only that which has been ordained for good will remain in the eternal calm and rest of heaven. This is the experience of those in that heavenly scene. You can also experience a foretaste of heaven, dear child of God, in the midst of your suffering as you heed the invitation of the Almighty to enter into His presence and pray. Please read the following: **Revelation 4:1-11; 7:9-17; 14:13; 21-22.**

Second, notice the guarantee, *"... I will answer thee..."* No prayer goes unheard or unanswered. When God makes and establishes a covenant, it will come to pass. *"God is not a man, that he should lie; neither the Son of Man, that he should repent: has he said, and shall he not do it? Or has he spoken, and shall he not make it good?"* (Numbers 23:19) *"And the Scripture cannot be broken."* (John 10:35)

While he was in prison, God admonished Jeremiah to call upon Him. Jeremiah continually experienced suffering in his life. But when the presence, power, and promise of God was infused into the process, the dynamics of suffering on earth for Jeremiah radically changed. As he prayed in faith in this temporal and physical realm, God gave to Jeremiah the guarantee that he would see some things, know some things, understand some things, experience some things, which otherwise he would have never seen, known, understood, or experienced had God not allowed him to go through his sufferings.

Third, notice the revelation, *"...and shew thee..."* We come to the results. In Jeremiah's life, all of these experiences would transcend him into the sphere of seeing and realizing *"...great and mighty things, which thou knowest not."* The glories of God and the secret place of our Lord in this life can only be realized through suffering. This will be a resounding theme as we continue. This *"knowest not"* concept can also be applicable in a negative sense. The suffering saint who does not follow through in faith with the concepts taught in **Jeremiah 33:3** will never know the peace, comfort, and all of the revelation that God desires to give of Himself in time of great need and peril.

The following verses lend credence and support that the promise of prayer supplies the specific need the suffering soul longs for in the days of adversity.

"The LORD is nigh unto all them that call *upon Him, to all that call upon Him in truth."* (Psalms 145:18) When we call upon God, we must recognize Him in the truth of His holiness and ourselves in the disparity of our depravity. We cannot hide anything from God, and we should never come to Him in pretense. We can come to God with all the ugliness of our emotions and just be real with Him. By embracing this truth we grow, develop, and mature in our Christian faith. He knows every failure

and all of our shortcomings, but He still loves us and invites us into His presence, so that we can be cared for and helped.

"The eyes of the LORD are upon the righteous, and his ears are open unto their cry." **(Psalms 34:15)** Our Lord sees all and He knows all. He sees you in that dark room all by yourself, loathing your condition, depressed by your circumstances and yearning for a favorable outcome. His ears hear your cry. Even when the articulation of your words has no discernible character. God even interprets the moaning of your heart, which manifests itself through the lamentation of your tears. *"For the LORD hath heard the voice of my weeping."* **(Psalms 6:8)** The very core of your agonies are interpreted through the utterance of your crying. You have gained access into the very presence of God because the gateway into His ears is open. His eyes see, and His ears hear. As we continue in prayer, we can know that we have open access to Him, confident that the Lord *"... heareth the cry of the afflicted."* **(Job 34:28)**

"And call upon Me in the day of trouble: I will deliver thee, *and thou shalt glorify Me"* *(*Psalms 50:15). Is the day of trouble at hand? So is the day of deliverance. Deliverance is not an "if" or "perhaps" or "maybe so." It's a definite oath given by the Almighty: *"I will deliver thee."* Therefore, you can persevere and never give up hope. Deliverance will come when the purpose of God is complete. In the process of time, His right arm will sustain you, and His countenance will lead you **(Psalms 4:6; 42:5; 44:3; 89:15)**.

"When I cry unto Thee, then shall mine enemies turn back: *this I know; for God is for me."* **(Psalms 56:9)** Do not entertain the thought for a moment that you are suffering because God is against you. This is a deception that the Wicked One will continually try to employ to keep you oppressed and in doubt of your Savior. *"If God be for us who can be against us?"* **(Romans 8:31)** In the New Testament, God never comes against His children in an adversarial way, but only in an advocating role **(Revelation 2:14, 20)**.

If the Lord chastens, He will do so because He loves His children. The chastening of the Lord is wrought to accomplish His desire to conform His children to the image of His Son, Jesus Christ **(Hebrews 12:5-8; Romans 8:29; Proverbs 3:11-13)**. It's great to know that your spouse, children, family, church and friends are for you. But there is no greater joy than to know God is for you! The whole world may turn against you, but Jesus is that "Friend that sticketh closer than a brother." **(Proverbs 18:24)**.

"They cried unto Thee, and were delivered: They trusted in Thee, and were not confounded." **(Psalms 22:5)** The promise of this verse teaches us that when we cry out to God, we don't have to be ashamed or disconcerted. When we call out to Him, we will never be disappointed that we did so. Do not take the low road of unbelief when you cry out to the Lord by saying, "He's not hearing or listening to me, because the answer has not yet come." He's intimately listening to your every word. He is engaged in thought towards you as He listens to your request. Your appeal will never fall on the deaf ears of God, because they do not exist. From the bow of the enemy will the arrow of negativity strike. But know this: the opposite of negativity is this truth: *"But verily God hath heard me; he hath attended to the voice of my prayer."* **(Psalms 66:19)** He's paying attention, close attention. Like the conductor who can hear every note of his symphony, even the sharp and flat notes, God hears the melodies of our sorrows, which come from the untuned strings of our heart. Just as God delivered His children in the past, He will deliver His children in the present and in the future. This is His promise.

"O LORD my God, I cried unto thee, and Thou hast healed me." **(Psalms 30:2)** *"Thou hast given him his heart's desire, and hast not withholden the request of his lips. Selah."* **(Psalms 21:2)** Many saints of God, even mature ones, become frustrated as they persevere in prayer, because they do not obtain the answer they are seeking in a timely manner. We must be careful when we approach God that we do not set a preconceived time limit, trying to bind God to our terms and conditions.

The expectation of faith and belief is greatly different than expecting God to do something according to our will. When this happens, thoughts of abandonment, doubt, and a sense that God is failing us will creep in. Job was depressed in his sufferings, not because he felt God was failing him.

He just did not understand. He was bewildered and shocked by the sudden rapidity of tragedies which struck his home.

Job was trying to make sense of it, but he could not. He was enveloped in confusion and filled with trepidation. I do not see in the book of Job (and I have analyzed it time and time again) where Job asked God to heal him. I find that strange and almost unexplainable. It seems to me that although Job was terribly suffering, he had a deep sense of awareness that God was moving and doing something in his life far beyond his comprehension.

In Job's own articulation we see the raw emotion of human agony and pain, but then we see his rare prevailing faith which believed God beyond his most difficult circumstances of life. Job, in a very bizarre way, teaches us the truth of **Psalms 37:4**, "Delight thyself also in the Lord; and he shall give thee the desires of thine heart." Our delights can lead to deception and many distractions, but His delights will transcend us to a sphere of greater and better desires, which are the desires of God. When we trade in our desires for God's desires, we can be sure that His desires can never be tainted. In Job's pain, this is what he was seeking, for he said, "Though he slay me, yet will I trust in him: but I will maintain mine own ways before him." **(Job 13:15)**

Job's unshakable, steadfast trust in God shows us that God's desire for Job's life, became far more important to Job, than Job's own desires for his life. When we go to God and pray in time of severe suffering, this lesson Job teaches us should become the end result of our thinking as we seek God for His blessings.

In this following story of praise, you're going to meet a remarkable woman who approached her life threatening crisis in the same manner as Job. She accepted the desire of God as His will for her life, and received from Him a wonderful revelation of His grace and power:

Two years ago today, I officially completed my cancer treatments and started this new journey of my life as a cancer survivor. This was the promise I held onto for that time and the God of all grace who called you to his eternal glory in Christ, after you have suffered a little while, will himself restore you and make you strong, firm and steadfast **(1 Peter 5:10).** *I learned:*

1. Surround yourself with prayer warriors. Growing up in the church, you are always taught to pray for others. A lot of times we feel selfish if we pray for ourselves, so during those insane months of diagnosis and treatment, there were times I was at a loss as to how to pray for myself.

That's when you so desperately depend on family and friends who love you and will intercede for you. I was fortunate to have people literally around the world praying for me and my family.

2. Stuff doesn't matter. It's okay if the dishes don't get done tonight. It's okay if I buy dessert for the party, instead of bringing homemade. What matters is people and the time you spend with them. I know it sounds like a cliche, but it's true. I want to see my kids grow up, get married, have kids of their own, and grow old with my husband. But if God brings me home before then, I want to have made my time on earth count. I want to fill my kids lives with love, experiences and laughter. And I want them to know that they matter and are more important than the dishes. I will continue on my new path as long as God allows and I will not just survive; I will thrive! My God is bigger than cancer. I will trust him and every day believe in my complete healing, because he promised to restore me!

Jill, a devoted wife and mother.

I love what she says: "I will not just survive; I will thrive!" This grace came to her, and the glories of this revelation occurred because she and others were praying!

"In that day when I cried Thou answeredst me, and strengthenedst me with strength in my soul."

(Psalms 138:3)

"Thou drewest near in the day that I called upon Thee: Thou saidst, fear not."

(Lamentations 3:57)

"When my soul fainted within me I remembered the LORD: and my prayer came in unto thee into Thine holy temple."

(JONAH 2:7)

When you consider all of the above verses concerning the promise of prayer, the conclusion you come to is that we can become complete. Notice the psalmist referenced the very day he called upon the Lord. That day became a memorial in his life, a source of reference, a clear indicator that God responded and began to move in the outward circumstances of his life. I am convinced that God moves the most when we call out to Him in our pain, suffering, fear, and time of conflict. We can have the confidence that God is never sitting idle in our day of trouble. Heaven is very active when the afflicted saint looks to the Savior, making an anguished plea for refuge.

Our fainting soul can be replenished, refreshed, renewed, restored, and revived! The soul which was weak and teetering, can now be filled with might and strength. Our trembling hearts can become fearless and courageous.

CHAPTER 13

The secret of suffering is found in

THE PROTECTION OF PRAYER

When we come to Christ, we are faced with the reality that our Christian experience and journey is likened unto warfare. The Christian walk is a daily battle, and at times can be a great struggle. It's good for the believer to learn this as early as possible. The fight is real and the warfare intense.

The following verses are very descriptive, teaching the Christian life is not a walk in the park, but rather a life spent in the middle of the ring, octagon, and cage, fighting a vicious opponent that is at all times our adversary and wanting to destroy us. Jesus told Peter that *"Satan hath desired to have you, that he may sift you as wheat."* (Luke 22:31)

"Be sober, be vigilant because your adversary the devil as a roaring lion walketh about seeking whom he may devour."

(1 PETER 5:8)

Jesus taught, "...The thief cometh but to steal, kill, and destroy..."

(JOHN 10:10)

The Apostle Paul taught young Timothy:

"Thou therefore, my son, be strong in the grace that is in Christ Jesus."

(2 TIMOTHY 2:1)

"Thou therefore endure hardness, as a good soldier of Jesus Christ. No man that warreth entangleth himself with the affairs of this life; that he may please Him who hath chosen him to be a soldier."

(2 TIMOTHY 2:3-4)

The language of the above verses are very graphic. In fact they are "R" rated for extreme violence and aggression. The enemy desires to "sift you." This means to completely separate you from your faith, confidence, trust, love, and desire for God. This is how wheat was sifted back in the time of Christ:

"The first step in the process of sifting wheat is to loosen the chaff from the edible grain, which is called threshing. The old-fashioned way to do this is to spread the wheat onto a floor made from stone, concrete, or tampered earth, and to beat it with a flail. The next step is called winnowing, where the loosened chaff is removed from the grain. The old-fashioned way of doing this was to throw the grain in the air, the lighter chaff would be blown off by even a decent breeze. The heavier grains would fall back to the ground below where they were thrown."

Jesus knew the enemy's attack would be vicious, and He prepared Peter by explaining that prayer would cause him to prevail.

A lion is a vicious wild animal. When these brutes of the jungle kill, they do so without mercy, ripping and tearing their prey into pieces. The lion will sink his sword-like teeth deep into the flesh of his victim: rending, disemboweling, and slaughtering the weaker creature, completely destroying life. The warning is serious "... seeking whom he may devour." There is no recovery for the prey which has been completely devoured by the lion!

Our adversary as a "thief" wants to rob us of joy, peace, and comfort. His intent is to kill all hope, and his motive is to deceive and to destroy your thought process, producing a negative, poisonous stream of hopelessness, helplessness, and bitter defeat.

We "endure hardness." That is, we persevere through the pain, and engage our hostile enemy on the battlefield of extreme spiritual warfare "... as a good soldier of Jesus Christ" through the grace of God that we find and obtain in the weapon of prayer.

One of the major tactics of the enemy is to try to destroy our faith and confidence in God. When the perserverance of faith is not embraced, casualties of faith are born out of trials of affliction.

Clamorous influences, like Job's wife, would implore us to "curse God and die" **(Job 2:9)** in our time of suffering. God forbid that we would become so weak and shipwrecked in our faith in time of trouble. Our Lord has given every weapon we need to prevail over any plight confronting us in the wilderness of this life: faith, the Holy Spirit, the encouragement of the family of God, and the weapon of prayer which protects us in time of battle.

Battle takes many forms. Suffering has many faces: sickness, temptation, severe offense, and torments of the mind. False teaching will lead the child of God to believe the Christian life is like a "banana-split" or a "bowl of cherries." The enemy has been a master at lulling the believer into a state of slumber, complacency, and lack of faith. These false teachers with their pernicious words will tell their audience, "With God the sun is always shining, the birds are always singing, the waters are always calm, the flowers are always blooming and the weather is always clement," but in reality the contrary and opposite may often be the case. Storms, trials, and valleys of life are far more frequent than the mountaintop experiences. These false teachers paint a portrait of God that once you come to the Lord, all conflicts, burdens and challenges will be no more. This reckless handling of the Word of God leaves many of God's children bewildered and confused, because even though trust and faith have been placed in the Lord, sorrows and struggles still remain and do not magically vanish or disappear.

God is not an antibiotic, a spare tire, or a microwave. God is not a "plop-plop, fizz-fizz, oh what a relief it is" answer to the maladies and trials of life. Yet, God has given to us everything we need to fight and win the battle. He does not leave us defenseless nor expose us to the elements of the world which would consume us in defeat. He is our rock, fortress, deliverer, strength, buckler, the horn of our salvation, and high tower **(Psalms 18:2)**.

Now let's consider the protection of prayer. Using graphic symbolism, **Ephesians 6:10-13** reveals that our Christian experience is likened unto aggressive, brutal, hand-to-hand combat! Our enemy, though, is not with flesh and blood (human), but rather with the deplorable forces of evil.

"Finally, my brethren, be strong in the Lord, and in the power of his might. Put on the whole armor of God, that ye may be able to stand against the wiles [trickery, subtle deceit] of the devil. For we wrestle not against flesh and blood, but against principalities [demonic forces that would desire to rule your life] against powers [demonic forces that would desire to influence your life] against the rulers of the darkness of this world, against spiritual wickedness in high places. Wherefore take unto you the whole armor of God, that ye may be able to withstand in the evil day, and having done all, to stand."

(EPHESIANS 6:10-13)

These verses teach that the mighty general of evil himself, the Devil, has his army and troops very well trained, organized, and strategically placed to do their battle with God's people. Our only complete protection is God's spiritual armor, which He has provided and has made available for all of His children. Every piece of His spiritual armor is put on by spending much time and effort in prayer: "Praying always with all prayer and supplication, and watching thereunto with all perseverance and supplication for all Saints." **(Ephesians 6:18)**

Putting on the whole armor of God is a daily experience and, in some cases, moment by moment. In essence, the nature of these weapons and clothing are both offensive and defensive. In **Ephesians 6:10-18**, the glaring detail jumping off the pages of this Scripture is as follows: tucked between the fact that we have a very formidable enemy, and that we must diligently give ourselves over to prayer, supplication, watching, and perseverance, is the mention of every piece of armor provided for the very survival of the believer. We must understand, beloved, though we experience our suffering in the natural, physical tangible realm, our greatest and most fierce battle and the true conflict is in the spiritual realm. "For we wrestle not against flesh and blood..." **(Ephesians 6:12a)** If we understand who and what our enemy really is, where he is, and how he works, then we can function and thrive. The geography of the battle is not the physical realm but the spiritual realm. The Christian soldier and sufferer must be trained to think this way.

When our thinking is correct, then our focus will be correct. When we get to this sphere and level of thought, it won't matter if we have the answers to our conflicts. What will matter is the truth which will sustain us through any conflict, which is the knowledge that the spiritual realm dictates, mandates, and controls the physical realm. By faith, we are made complete in Christ. When we can see this, and only this, it will be then that the physical, natural, and tangible world, in which we live, will become as a grain of sand in our thinking in comparison to the universe of God's spiritual realm where nothing can touch, hurt, or harm us! When you decide to live in God's supernatural realm by faith, you will become a "giant killer," and nothing in this world will be able to rob you of the joy of the Lord or keep you from His comfort and the peace that passeth all understanding.

We are told to have our "loins girt about with truth." **(Ephesians 6:14a)** Seeking God in truth, walking with God in truth, and having truth as the main core value and foundation of our relationship with our Lord, is an imperative and means everything.

"The LORD is nigh unto all them that call upon him, to all that call upon him in truth."

(PSALMS 145:18)

101

"God is a Spirit: and they that worship him must worship him in spirit and in truth."

(John 4:24)

Paul had much experience in dealing with Roman soldiers. He often was escorted by them into prisons because of his love, obedience, and faithfulness to God. The Apostle Paul was also a Roman citizen, and no doubt was exposed to the Roman culture and soldier on a daily basis. It was the duty of the Roman warrior to keep peace and act as the "police" of the Roman Empire. Roman soldiers were woven into the very fabric of the community life at Rome.

One of the most important parts of the Roman soldier's uniform was an undergarment which supported the entire midsection area, front to back. Think of it as a big, thick belt that wrapped around the entire waist. This offered tremendous support and balance in battle. In exercise science, you are only as strong as the area of your body known as the abdominal muscles and its antagonist, your lower back; this is your "core." Every other area of your fitness development depends on the core. The stronger the core, the better equipped the athlete will be! Truth is the rock, pillar, cornerstone and foundation of our entire Christian system. Jesus said, "I am the way, the truth, and the life." **(John 14:6) He also said,** "And ye shall know the truth and the truth shall set you free." **(John 8:32)** The psalmist David said, "... thou desirest truth in the inward parts..." **(Psalms 51:6)** David's prayer and statement to God, was his profound desire be the same in the public eye, as he was in private.

Only a life of "truth" can produce this. Why is "truth" an important factor in our suffering? The first piece of armor that God instructs us to put on through prayer is "absolute truth." In our time of suffering, there may be a certain truth or truths God wants us to understand and know. Suffering is like a refining fire, the furnace of our Lord, or being "tried with fire." It burns the dross of self-deception out of our life **(1 Peter 1:7)**. It is said that the refiner of gold will continue to cause the precious metal to pass through the fire until his own reflection can be seen. Suffering conforms us into the very image of Jesus Christ. This is what Paul meant when he said, "That I may know him, and the power of his resurrection, and the fellowship of his sufferings, being made conformable unto his death." In **2 Peter 4:1-2** we find one of the most remarkable verses in all of God's Word: "For as much then as Christ hath suffered for us in the flesh, arm yourselves likewise with the same mind: for he that hath suffered in the flesh hath ceased from sin; that he no longer should live the rest of his time in the flesh to the lust of men, but to the will of God." Christ suffered because He is truth.

Our Lord is the personification of Truth. There is no guile, falsehood or deceit in Him. He is called "The faithful witness." **(Revelation 1:5)** He was despised and rejected because He revealed the truth of the Heavenly Father. He gave the truth that transforms and changes lives. When God allows us to suffer, we tend to see things more clearly. Suffering has a way of causing introspection. It compels us to look into the deep recesses of our soul. When we finally have the courage to look there, being honest with ourselves, and in our minds we go to that place and stand before the doors to the chambers of our heart, where we have locked and hidden away secrets known only to God and self. We want no one else to go into these small rooms, because we are too fearful and insecure to separate ourselves from the carnal pleasures which we have tucked away.

When God allows suffering to come into our lives, this puts us on an island of self-contemplation. This compels us to begin opening those fortified rooms, and allows the Holy Spirit to clean out those compartments and refurnish them with truth. Do not be confused or troubled. This process of God is not the reason for our suffering, but the sweet reward or by-product of our suffering.

Those who willfully and presumptuously sin and bring upon themselves the natural consequences resulting from their rebellious and disobedient choices, can also enter into this blessing of our Lord's refining fire. Thus, suffering provides a catalyst to conform the repentant and restored soul into the image of Jesus Christ, God's Son. God's purpose for His children is that we be conformed into the image of His dear Son, Jesus our Lord **(Romans 8:29)**.

The next piece of armor guards and develops our heart: "And having on the breastplate of righteousness." **(Ephesians 6:14b)**

This breastplate of righteousness is also called in scripture the "armor of righteousness" **(2 Corinthians 6:7)** and is only obtainable through prayer and obedience. When we put on God's breastplate and armor of righteousness by faith, this will create in you the boldness of a lion **(Proverbs 28:1)**.

The breastplate was a vital piece in the coat of mail (suit of armor) for the Roman warrior. It protected the upper body, particularly the heart and lungs of the soldier. This breastplate of righteousness tied into and overlapped the belt of truth, which secured the waist and the midsection. The spiritual application of this "breastplate of righteousness" reveals the importance of protecting our hearts from the ungodliness of this world.

Righteousness will always increase and develop as a by-product of suffering. Our internal thinking will change, which will manifest itself in our outward conduct. When we suffer, we tend to see the world differently. Our hearts become more sensitive and tender to the world and others around us. Suffering also motivates us to seek more truth, which tempers that breastplate of righteousness and makes it harder and harder to be influenced by the corruption and false philosophies of the world. "Create in me a clean heart, O God; and renew a right spirit within me" **(Psalms 51:10)**.

Spiritual heart surgery belongs to the Lord only. Often, though, it is suffering which drives us to this Great Physician. Suffering helps us to look inward, to self-inspect, to analyze and evaluate our intent and motives. When we do this, it creates humility, meekness, and righteousness. *"Seek ye the LORD, all ye meek of the earth, which have wrought his judgment; seek righteousness, seek meekness: it may be ye shall be hid in the day of the LORD'S anger."* (Zephaniah 2:3)

Suffering is a great motivator, which compels us to follow after and seek to emulate the virtuous moral attributes of God: "But thou, O man of God, flee these things; and follow after righteousness, godliness, faith, love, patience, meekness." **(1 Timothy 6:11)**; "Flee also youthful lusts: but follow, faith, charity, peace, with them that call on the LORD out of a pure heart." **(2 Timothy 2:22)** Suffering also creates a hunger and thirst for righteousness, but notice the outcome—blessedness and happiness. "Blessed are they which do hunger and thirst after righteousness: for they shall be filled." **(Matthew 5:6)**

Righteous suffering is a great beacon of light, hope, and encouragement for those who know not the Lord. The magnetic pull that suffering generates is incalculable! "And your feet shod with the preparation of the gospel of peace..." **(Ephesians 6:15)** Between 30 and 100 A.D. the early church shared and exposed the whole known world, at that time, to the gospel of Jesus Christ! This was all accomplished through severe suffering and persecution under the tyranny of Nero and Domitian **(Romans 10:18; Colossians 1:6, 23)**.

The light that you shine in the midst of your suffering has a powerful influence. Lest we forget, it was the passion and suffering of Christ which saved the world. When our daughter Lindsay went through her battle with cancer, she was filled with joy, peace, and comfort from the Heavenly Father. The way she conducted herself spoke volumes for our Lord and His truth. She let her light *"so shine before men."* And it was unmistakable that His supernatural presence was upon her, influencing all who were exposed to her for the gospel. Suffering in the life of a believer is its own unique megaphone which makes loud and clear the message of the gospel for all to witness and hear **(Romans 10:14)**.

Often, suffering does bring sorrow and grief. When we are suffering and in pain, God is not expecting us to walk around with a pretend smile or an outward persona that mocks the reality of our suffering. We *"Sorrow not, even as others which have no hope."* **(1 Thessalonians 4:13)** Often a quiet resolve and internal strength reveals itself through calmness and the quietness of our spirit which responds to hostile outward attacks with a persevering and prevailing faith.

This is the manner in which Job suffered. People saw his pain, anguish, depression, fear, and perplexity. But paralleling these outward emotions of despair, they also saw in Job unyielding, undying, immovable steadfast love, devotion, loyalty and respect for the Lord. This evident character of Job was indisputable, for God declared of him to the Devil, "Hast thou considered my servant Job, that there is none like him in the earth, a perfect and and upright man, one that fearest God, and escheweth evil?" **(Job 1:8)** If God saw this in Job, so did everyone else who saw and knew him. The only ones who doubted Job were his self-righteous friends. God reproved them for this and vindicated His servant Job. When you read the book of Job, your heart breaks for this man, because of the indescribable pain which he endured. But you also see a giant of the faith who continued to believe and honor God throughout the whole course of his bitter journey.

In **Ephesians 6:19-20**, Paul asked the church of Ephesus to pray for him that he would have the boldness to speak, preach, and teach the gospel of Jesus Christ. Also, the disciples had great power on the day of Pentecost to preach and share the gospel, because they had spent much time in one accord together in the unity of suffering and in the harmony of prayer **(Acts 1:14; 2:1-41)**.

"They that sow in tears shall reap in joy. He that goeth forth and weepeth, *bearing precious seed, shall doubtless come again with rejoicing, bringing his sheaves with him."* **(Psalms 126:5-6)** Sowing in tears and weeping refers not only to the burden of prayers being offered for those who do not know the Lord, but it also refers to those who sorrowfully suffer and still have enough compassion and love for the unsaved to share their faith, even in the midst of their own personal storms. The early church was the greatest example of this, through many years of persecution and suffering.

Suffering is the greatest force, motivator, and mover for the gospel. Nothing compels the lost more than observing children of God who continue to love, worship, serve, and testify of the goodness of God in the midst of their own personal storm of affliction.

From 590 to 1517 AD, the period known as the "dark ages," over 50 million believers suffered horrifically for their faith. Many were burned at the stake, imprisoned, or tortured to death. Multitudes during this time turned to the Lord, because they saw in these courageous believers a supernatural peace and comfort and a steadfast resolve, which can only come from grace abounding in the souls of the saints who suffered in faith. In handling the Word of God for more than thirty years, I've seen more people come to Christ as a result of those who wore the gospel shoes, treading through the deep valleys of despair, as they remained a true gospel witness through their own perilous times.

The footwear of the Roman soldier provided swiftness and agility during battle. The proper protection for the feet also ensured a readiness for the combatant to engage in the battle at a moment's notice. These war shoes assured great maneuverability and balance as the combatant defended his empire in the fiercest of conflicts. The Bible describes the feet of the soul-winner as something of great beauty, because they are responsible for delivering the message of hope **(Isaiah 52:7; Romans 10:14-15)**. Suffering has a way of trying to knock us down and out. Not so for the believer; the message of the gospel is our stability and hope!

"Above all taking the shield of faith..."

(EPHESIANS 6:16)

When our Lord was in His earthly ministry, the disciples asked of Him to increase their faith **(Luke 17:5)**. The only way that we can overcome the world (everything that attacks from without), flesh (ourselves), the devil (our constant foe), and please God is through faith. The Apostle Paul instructed young Timothy that the only way he could fight a good warfare was by embracing the weapon of faith. Not only did the shield of the Roman soldier protect him from flying arrows, wielded swords, and the piercing of spears, but it also was used as an offensive weapon. The shield, when used skillfully, could knock out or even kill an opponent with its crushing blows.

This shield of our faith will absorb all the mighty blows of our enemy. The shield of faith will cover and protect us from every ill emotion which would try to penetrate our soul. Behind the shield, we are beyond the enemy's reach. With the shield out front, we can still feel the intensity of the battle. We can see its ugly sights, hear its frightening sounds, smell its foul odors, and taste its bitter portion. But distress will not be our captor. Despair will not be our guide. Distraction will not be our stumbling block.

Defeat will not be our end, and death will never conquer! Why? Because when the shield of faith is out in front, nothing can overcome it. **FAITH** overcomes all!

Listen to the words of the Apostle Paul as he describes in detail the intensity of the conflict: "We are troubled on every side, yet not distressed; we are perplexed, but not in despair; persecuted, but not forsaken; cast down, but not destroyed; always bearing about in the body the dying of the Lord Jesus, that the life also of Jesus might be made manifest in our body. For we which live are always delivered unto death for Jesus' sake, that the life also of Jesus might be made manifest in our mortal flesh. So then death worketh in us [suffering, conflict, and challenges] but life in you [the benefits and blessings that others will experience as they witness your good conversation and faithful testimony]. We have the same spirit of faith ..." **(2 Corinthians 4:8-13a)**

Did you catch that last line? "We have the same spirit of faith..." This faith, my friend, is the faith that overcomes the world **(1 John 5:4-5)**, which means there is nothing in this world that can overtake your faith! How powerful is the shield of faith? It is impenetrable, which means we will always prevail through any suffering we might face. To God be the glory! Blessed be to His holy name!

A final thought on the shield of faith. "Above all, taking the shield of faith, wherewith ye shall be able to quench all the fiery darts of the wicked." **(Ephesians 6:16)** These "fiery darts" are skillfully guided missiles or arrows from the enemy. He knows your every frailty, weakness, and fear. He knows exactly where to aim. He will aim at your worry, stresses of the unknown, and the imagination. He will aim at your thoughts of the future, and shoot as many arrows of negative thoughts at you at one time as he possibly can. Though we may feel the blows of these arrows and missiles upon our shield, with our shield we will be able to deflect or quench them and continue to move forward being victorious in every battle of life by faith!

"And take the helmet of salvation, and the sword of the Spirit, which is the word of God."

(EPHESIANS 6:17)

Each piece of armor is vital and integral to the whole, but the helmet and the sword are perhaps two of the most important pieces because the one protects the head (the helmet) and the other (the sword) protects both offensively and defensively. The Roman sword had many purposes. It was an emblem of strength, power, and protection. Spiritually, both the helmet and the sword are most effective when put on and applied through prayer.

The fundamental principle taught in any fighting system is to always keep your guard up and protect your head. My kickboxing coach used to say, "If your lights go out, you're done!" Meaning, don't get knocked out. The helmet of salvation and the sword of the Spirit through prayer are great protections for the mind, soul, body, and spirit, providing support, satisfaction, supply, strength, and everything needed for success in the battles and sufferings of life.

Earlier In our discussion on this passage of Scripture **(Ephesians 6:10-13)** we saw how important right thinking is when it comes to the matters of the conflicts, challenges and sufferings we face in life. In His Word, God has given to us over 7000 "Exceeding great and precious promises." **(2 Peter 1:4)** Some of His promises are unconditional, like the promise of salvation, His soon and imminent return, the establishment of the new heaven and the new earth, and the promise that one day He will destroy and put down all sin and evil, and incarcerate the devil for all of eternity into the bottomless pit **(John 3:16; 6:37; Philippians 1:6; 1 Thessalonians 4:13-18; 1 Corinthians 15:52-58; Revelation 20:1-3, 10; 21:1-7; 2 Peter 3:8-13)**.

Many other promises in God's Word are, in fact, very conditional. Meaning, if we obey His Word, yield and submit to it, and by faith believe and embrace His promises, He will then fulfill in us the promises of His Word. The following verses are just a select few which carry in them great weight, effectiveness, and power, if we believe them and trust in them.

"Thou wilt keep him in perfect peace, whose mind is stayed on

thee: because he trusteth in thee." (Isaiah 26:3) "Perfect peace..." What can interrupt perfect peace? Not *"tribulation, or distress, or persecution, or famine, or nakedness, or peril or sword... Neither death, nor life, nor angels, nor principalities, nor powers, nor things present, nor things to come, nor height, nor depth, nor any other creature..." (Romans 8:35, 38-39)* There is not a medication, a philosophy, any psychological professional, a song, an organization, a support group, or any worldly component which can bring or give *"perfect peace."* This perfect peace is endowed to the believer as his or her mind is fixed on the Lord. Something that is perfect has no instability or futility. This perfect peace is not in a place of mystery. It is not a lost treasure which has to be searched for or found. It's a piece of armor which must be put on through prayer. Prayer brings hope, peace, and promise beyond the present tense circumstances of life.

CONFORMING VERSUS TRANSFORMING

We must work on our thought process. This takes training and discipline. Our Lord gives us His master plan so the heavenly perfect peace can be fulfilled in us. The following verses will show us our responsibility in the matter and also reveal the wonderful provision of God for our mental and emotional stability, no matter what our infirmities may be.

"Be not conformed to this world: but be ye transformed by the renewing of your mind, that ye may prove what is that good, and acceptable, and perfect, will of God." (Romans 12:2) The world and its philosophies and ways has influenced the thinking of the majority of believers. What we see, feel, and experience with our senses causes real bondage for the soul and great conflict for the mind. The language at the beginning of this verse is very strange to me. This tells me, at the point of conversion, God gives to every believer the mind of Christ. Our thinking will automatically change as the Holy Spirit moves faster than the speed of light to reconfigure the mind of the newly born child of God.

God's influence upon the mind at conversion is a very illuminating and overwhelming procedure. So, immediately, at the new birth, the epic battle of conforming versus transforming begins! This will be a lifelong struggle. The world with its carnal, magnetic pull viciously begins to tug and attempt to take over, desiring to route and control the mind of the new believer. Therefore, the immediate instruction given by God is to "Be not conformed...But be ye transformed." For the believer, there are two major influences: **God** or the **World.** Continual transformation will take place as we set, fix, and seek to meditate, peruse, and muse on the character of Christ and the love of God. When we set our affections on Him, we will then know and experience the perfect peace of heaven **(Psalms 1:1-2; 119:97)**.

For God hath not given us the spirit of fear; but of power, and of love and of a sound mind." **(2 Timothy 1:7)** In the King James version of Bible, we are told 103 times to *"fear not"* or *"be not afraid."* Fear is spoken of over 500 times in the King James Bible, and often, it refers to the fear and reverence we should have for the Lord. This fear works in our favor, because if we have a rightful fear and respect for God, this would cause us not to fear anything else. Why? When God is feared, we then recognize and realize His enormity and superiority over everything. This fear teaches us that God is incomparable. Therefore, no threat that comes into our life is bigger or can overcome the God we love, serve, and trust. The acrostic for fear can be stated this way:

- **False**
- **Evidence**
- **Appearing**
- **Real**

Much of what we fear will never come to pass. Fear and worry is like a rocking chair, it will consume 90% of your time and energy but you will never get anywhere.

"Be careful for nothing; but in everything by prayer and supplication with thanksgiving let your requests be made known unto God."

(PHILIPPIANS 4:6)

"And the peace of God, which passeth all understanding, shall keep your hearts and minds *through Christ Jesus."*

(PHILIPPIANS 4:7)

"Finally, brethren, whatsoever things are true, whatsoever things are honest, whatsoever things are just, whatsoever things are pure, whatsoever things are lovely, whatsoever things are of good report; if there be any virtue, and if there be any praise, think on these things."

(PHILIPPIANS 4:8)

"For the weapons of our warfare are not carnal [sinful or of the natural realm], but mighty through God to the pulling down of strongholds [that thing which would bind, hinder, thwart, impede or incarcerate]; Casting down imaginations, and every high thing that exalteth itself against the knowledge of God, and bringing into captivity every thought to the obedience of Christ."

(2 CORINTHIANS 10:4-5)

The five verses of Scripture that make up this passage are like a fortress for the soul. These verses are a G.P.S. (global positioning system)—a road map—to perfect peace. We could call this process **"God's piloting system."** We don't know what God knows. We cannot see what God sees. The revelation of His will is always progressive. In this world we can feel very lost and alone, especially when we find ourselves in the thick, dark forest of suffering.

These last two vital pieces of the armor, **the helmet** (which protects) and **the sword** (which procures) are really the foundation for all of the other pieces. Let me explain: with our mind, we choose to put on the belt of truth, to declare the message of truth, God's saving grace. With our mind we choose to take up the shield of faith, and to guard our heart we take up the breastplate of righteousness. Everything starts in the mind: our reason, logic, feelings and emotions. This is why every thought should be captured by thinking, "Lord, how can I please, honor, glorify, and satisfy You in my life?"

This can only be accomplished in the mind, through much diligent time spent in that secret place, sanctuary, garden of intimacy, fellowship and communion called "prayer." The helmet of salvation completes the process and unifies all the other pieces of the spiritual armor into one unstoppable heavenly weapon, which can defeat any evil foe on the planet. The armor protects everything from without and from within. When the helmet of salvation is truly put on, this will cause and create in us the fulfillment of the verses we've just considered in our study. Here is how we apply the helmet of salvation: it must be put on through the process of prayer!

The moment we remove the sword of the Spirit from its sheath by faith and look into the perfect law of liberty (God's Word), all the other pieces of our spiritual armor will activate, giving us all of their benefits simultaneously. "For the Word of God is quick [to do its work within the soul], and powerful [for in it is harnessed the omnipotence of God], and sharper than any two-edged sword, piercing even to the dividing asunder of soul and spirit, and of joints and marrow, and is a discerner of the thoughts and intents of the heart." **(Hebrews 4:12)** The Word of God is the conduit through which every benefit and blessing of our Lord will flow into our lives. Through prayer and meditation upon the Word of God, our Lord will create new neurological pathways in the brain, thus transforming our minds!

CHAPTER 14

The secret of suffering

THE PEOPLE FOR WHOM
WE SHOULD PRAY

"Praying for others is the foundation, pillar, and cornerstone of real ministry."

"I exhort therefore, that, first of all, supplications, prayers, intercessions, and giving of thanks, be made for all men; For kings, and for all that are in authority; that we may lead a quiet and peaceable life in all godliness and honesty."

(1 TIMOTHY 2:1-2)

Look what prayer yields: ***"a quiet and peaceable life."*** When we enter into a world of prayer, we then pray for the world. This is a very powerful essential as we wade in the ocean of our suffering. This is the principle I call "living outside of self" that we might serve, help, and care for others.

I once heard a story of a woman who was just given a very short time to live — just a matter of days. As she contemplated her imminent fate, she thought within herself, *"What must I do with my final hours?"* She made a conscious decision that she would live out the rest of her days helping and serving others. So day after day she preoccupied herself with giving and caring for the needs of those around her.

Days went by, then weeks, and finally months. Then someone close to her finally asked the question, "Were you not given the news you were supposed to die in just a matter of days?" When she stopped long enough to think about this profound question, her answer was quite astonishing. "I was so intensely focused on helping others, I guess I just forgot to die." This woman went on to live a long and fruitful life. Prayer helps us to do this very thing: minister to others in their time of need.

THIS TYPE OF PRAYING WILL KEEP US FROM SPIRITUAL DROUGHT IN OUR LIFE

As we pray for others to be comforted, we, ourselves, will be comforted too. Prayerlessness is the dam which will stop the flow of God's blessings to and through you. A life without prayer does not just affect self; it will also leave your family, friends, and all of mankind everywhere wanting and in need. The scope of your prayers will reach to the ends of the earth.

How powerful is prayer? Prayer can reach and influence the entire populated globe...that's power! The kind of praying that will help us in our time of need, is not a shallow, superficial, baby powder on the skin, perfume form of praying. Real prayer is labor intensive.

This section of our study on the subject matter of suffering is not meant to be an indictment on a weak prayer life, but rather an encouragement as to how we can rise above the clouds of our own suffering and encourage ourselves in the Lord as we encourage others through prayer. Remember we said earlier in our study, that supplication is the very soul of prayer: pleading, beseeching, imploring and earnestly asking with fervent desire and burden for that one thing greatly needed, a need intensely felt. Intercession is forgetting ourselves and praying for people in their need. Suffering believers would have a full-time ministry, if they were diligently and continuously praying for others. Job offered sacrifice and prayed for his children daily and continually **(Job 1:5).**

Intercessory prayer should be offered up for immediate family and especially for our children.

"And Abram said, Lord God, what wilt thou give me, seeing I go childless, and the steward of my house is this Eliezer of Damascus?"

"And Abram said, behold, to me thou hast given no seed: and, lo, one born in my house is mine heir."

(GENESIS 15:2-3)

"And Abraham said unto God, O that Ishmael might live before thee!"

(GENESIS 17:18)

Abraham was concerned about the fulfillment of the covenant, the promise God had given to him that his seed would be raised up in multitude as the stars of heaven. Abraham had to persevere in this promise, believe this promise, and wait upon God for the fulfillment of this promise. In the process of time, he earnestly prayed about these family matters and talked much with God about them **(Genesis 15:1-6; 17:1-22; 18:1-14).**

Another great example of steadfast, aggressive praying for family is seen in this Canaanite woman, who was a grieving, desperate mother:

"And, behold, a woman of Canaan came out of the same coasts, and cried unto Him, saying, Have mercy on me, O Lord, thou son of David; my daughter is grievously vexed with the devil."

(MATTHEW 15:22)

When faithful intercession is offered for our children, we help protect and shield them from the enemy. This Canaanite woman, in her pain, sought the Lord and prayed earnestly. She did plead with God that her daughter would be made whole and rescued from the clutches of the evil one **(Matthew 15:22-28)**. This woman was probably suffering as a result of her own poor choices in life. She failed to bring her daughter up in *"the nurture and admonition of the Lord."* **(Ephesians 6:4)** As a result, the daughter was *"grievously vexed with a devil."* The only hope for this mother was Jesus! She besought the Lord with a passionate and unyielding pursuit for her daughter (intercessory prayer) and God heard her prayer and delivered the child. A praying mother or father provides for their children an invaluable spiritual wealth, which far exceeds any material gain. When we engage in intercessory prayer for our close family members, as we suffer, our care for them will take the focus off our own cares. As a natural byproduct of our focus on the prayer needs of our family, our own burdens will be lifted and comfort will be imputed to our souls.

Intercessory prayer should be offered up for our friends

"Therefore take unto you now seven bullocks and seven rams, and go to my servant Job, and offer up for yourselves a burnt offering; and my servant Job shall pray for you; for him will I accept: lest I deal with you after your folly, in that ye have not spoken of me the thing which is right, like my servant Job."

(JOB 42:8)

Job prayed for his three friends who falsely accused him of cursing before the Lord. God wonderfully responded to the prayer of Job for his friends. Not only were his friends blessed and spared from judgment, but Job was greatly blessed both inwardly and outwardly because of his faithful work of intercessory prayer.

"And the LORD turned the captivity of Job, when he prayed for his friends: also the LORD gave Job twice as much as he had before."

(JOB 42:10)

As we pray for our friends in the midst of our suffering, this will help us as well as help them. I have found that the greatest way to minister to yourself is to minister to others. God will touch them, as well as touch you. I don't put much importance on feelings, because God does not. In the Word of God the Bible does not say anything about living by our feelings, because it's all about living by our faith. The Word of God does talk about our rejoicing, praising and thanksgiving **(Philippians 4:4-6; 1 Thessalonians 5:18)**. These expressions, I know, stem from good feelings, as we give praise and thanks to God for His bountiful blessings. These good and wholesome feelings are produced through our faith.

We must be careful though, not to get these priorities and progressions confused. Feelings and emotions are a big part of life, but they must be in proper perspective and in their right place lest they cause confusion. Listen to the Apostle Paul as he sits in prison in a time of his own personal suffering. He is ministering to the Philippian Church and he says something astonishing to them.

"Yea, and if I be offered upon the sacrifice and service of your faith, I joy, and rejoice with you all. For the same cause also do ye joy, and rejoice with me."

(PHILIPPIANS 4:17-18)

The byproduct of Paul feeling better and being comforted in his time of severe trial and suffering, came through the fact that he was praying and ministering to others.

Intercessory prayer should be offered up for all saints

"Praying always with all prayer and supplication in the spirit, and watching thereunto with all perseverance and supplication for all saints."

(EPHESIANS 6:18)

This next truth is closely related to the prayer essential we just considered. We have a duty and responsibility to pray for our brothers and sisters in Christ. Notice, the word **"watching"** is added to the ingredients of prayer. This almost makes the elixir of prayer complete. Watching is a very important component of prayer. To watch means to be alert, on guard, discerning, and sensitive. There are so many prayer needs that surround us daily. The average Christian, though, is dull in spiritual alertness. Self-centeredness and the overwhelming affinity with temporal gratification causes multitudes of those professing Christianity to lose sight of and to never take hold of the most important ministry of prayer **(Colossians 3:1-3)**.

All one must do is to stop, look, and listen to be made aware of the masses of hurting humanity, especially within the body of believers, who so desperately need the ministry of prayer. In our suffering, this type of prayer ministry can become a glorious and a very fulfilling spiritual endeavor and experience. The great truth is this: when we minister to others in this way, for the honor and glory of God, the natural byproduct and outcome of this is that we will be ministering to ourselves as well. The Spirit of God will minister to our hearts and comfort our souls as we diligently seek in prayer, supplication, and earnest desire the comfort, healing, and blessings for others. In prayer you will definitely reap what you sow **(Galatians 6:7)**.

For the Apostle Paul and his ministry team, this was common practice. Listen to his powerful words as he writes to the Corinthian believers, "Blessed be God, even the father of our Lord Jesus Christ, the father of all mercies and the God of all comfort; who comforteth us in all our tribulation, that we may be able to comfort them which are in any trouble, by the comfort wherewith we ourselves are comforted of God. For as the sufferings of Christ abound in us, so our consolation also aboundeth by Christ. And whether we be afflicted, it is for your consolation and salvation, which is effectual in the enduring of the same sufferings which we also suffer: or whether we be comforted, it is for your consolation and salvation. And our hope of you is stedfast, knowing, that as ye are partakers of the sufferings, so shall ye be also of the consolation." **(2 Corinthians 1:3-7)**

No secular-humanist psychologist, psychiatrist, or counselor, using the wisdom of this world, can compare or even begin to comprehend the wealth of spiritual and emotional wholeness that the triad of these truths can supply. Paul begins his statements by sentiments of praise as he blesses the Lord. Paul could praise God in this manner because he himself had received the wonderful blessing of the comforts of God.

Notice, Paul did not say that God had comforted him in some, or even in most, of his tribulation, but "in all our tribulation." The Apostle Paul received and experienced this comfort in times of severe conflict and was able to provide it for others through a strong outward testimony of intercessory prayer for the saints. This passage indicates that the more Paul suffered, the greater consolation that others received and experienced through his outward ministry towards them. What we see here is a beautiful circle of blessing. The sufferers are comforted, and they bring comfort to those who are suffering. In turn, those who are suffering as they are comforted bring comfort to the very same people who sought to comfort them in their time of affliction.

INTERCESSORY PRAYER SHOULD BE OFFERED UP FOR ALL MEN

We are commanded to pray for people everywhere. Prayer is faster, quicker, and far more reaching than any satellite or computer. How do you pray for the world? Pray for the hungry, needy, oppressed, persecuted, sick, hurting and suffering. Pray for countries, states, cities and towns. Pray that God would reveal Himself to save the broken and seeking heart. **The prayer of faith can blanket the entire world, providing a warmth and comfort to mankind!** Unknown to you in this life, but revealed in the life to come, will be the scope, benefit and testament of your praying obedience. Only eternity itself will bare the evidenced fruit of faithful praying for all of mankind! In your own time of suffering, as you minister to the world through prayer, I pray the following truths would bring revival to your soul and encouragement to your heart.

There are two heavenly scenes in the book of Revelation where the **"prayers of the saints"** are mentioned. The first reference is in relation to the opening of the seven-sealed book. The Holy Lamb of God is the only one worthy to open and loose the seals thereof. The contents of the seven-sealed book reveal the destiny and judgment of the earth and its inhabitants. Only the sovereign Savior, the Lamb of God, the One who holds the keys of hell and of death **(Revelation 1:18),** in whom all dominions, kingdoms, peoples, nations, languages, angels, principalities, authorities, powers are made subject unto Him, is worthy to open the book and loose the seals thereof **(Revelation 5:5)**. In this heavenly scene, we see that Christ hath prevailed! He overcame death, the grave, hell, sin, and Satan.

The opening of the seven-sealed book gives us a glimpse into the second most pivotal event in world history. This marks the judgment of all mankind, the false religious systems of the world, the corrupt military systems of the world, the dishonest economic systems of the world, Satan, the Antichrist, and the False Prophet. This seven-sealed book represents the title deed to all of the earth and all of the events that are about to unfold upon the earth **(Revelation 6, 17, 18, 19, and 20)**.

As the Apostle John witnesses the heavenly majestic scene of the Lion of the Tribe of Judah taking the book out of the right hand of Him (God) who sits upon the throne, he sees the four beasts and the four and twenty elders fall down before the Lamb to worship and praise. John notices that the elders are holding vials (bowls) full of odors (incense) "...which are the prayers of saints." **(Revelation 5:8)**

These prayers are the earthly prayers of God's people for all of mankind. They have been stored, saved, and collected in vials (bowls). The odors (incense) of these prayers have been a sweet-smelling savor in the nostrils of God, and show us that His senses (His heart, mind, power, and will) responded to the faithful praying of His people. Notice, the prayer of the saints in **verse 8** of **Revelation chapter 5** is directly linked to the multitudes of the redeemed (those who have been bought back by the precious blood of Jesus Christ) "...out of every kindred and tongue, and people, and nation..." **(Revelation 5:9-11)**

The prayer of the saints mentioned in Revelation chapter 5 is placed in the text before the opening of the seven-sealed book in Revelation chapter 6. Why? Because as a result of the faithful praying of God's people, God is now going to move and bring to pass His divine counsels. His eternal purpose for the world will now unfold. Revelation chapter 6 gives us a glimpse into this glorious future event. I want you to notice the divine link between the eternal purposes of God and the faithful praying of God's people to bring to fruition His great plan for the ages. God, in His goodness, allows His people to partner with Him in His most holy and eternal work. This happens through the wonderful opportunity, ability and ministry of prayer!

The second reference to the **"prayers of all saints"** in **Revelation 8:3-4** is in relation to God's judgment, that is, making "right" all of the "wrongs" of injustice. These prayers are escorted with much incense within the golden censer and carried right into the very presence of God, into the Holy of Holies, and placed on the golden altar before His throne. These are the prayers **"of all saints."** Therefore, this event is not limited or isolated to the time of the tribulation period only.

The prayers of all saints for all of mankind has a great part in fulfilling the eternal purpose of Christ, which will be realized in us throughout all of eternity, as we experience all the fullness of God **(Ephesians 3:11, 13)**. The prayers that we pray for world peace, and to understand the tragic mysteries of life, will one day be revealed to us with full enlightenment and knowledge **(1 Corinthians 13:12)**.

The ministry of personal prayer in our time of suffering is an unexplainable and undefinable strength to the soul. The simple explanation is this: when we pray for others to be helped, we ourselves are helped by the same token or measure wherewith our faith has extended to those in need. We often think of giving to be done only in the physical realm, with God reciprocating back to us His blessings. In reality, we can invest ourselves in God's spiritual temple of prayer, this Holy of Holies, where the incense of the Spirit of God continually emanates upward, filling the very throne room and touching His very heart!

In **Philippians 2:25-30**, the Apostle Paul tells the story and gives the testimony of a man by the name of Epaphroditus. This man was sick and near death; to say the least, he was suffering. The great characteristic of this man's life in his time of severe personal struggle is that he took his own thoughts and focus off himself and instead ministered to those around him. The Bible tells us that "God had mercy on him." The greatest example of this for me personally is my spiritual father, Doug "Dad" Robertson. Dad is an amazing saint of God. I also call him my "prayer angel." Dad Robertson will pray for anyone, at any time, in any place! I have been with him in restaurants and watched as he would approach and engage every person in his path with a kind word and a loving touch. It would not be long after the brief encounter, that all heads would be bowed in the middle of that public place, and a prayer meeting would ensue for the needy.

Dad's ministry is prayer. Most people will never know, as Dad labors in prayer, that he himself is in much physical pain and discomfort. He prays for people all over the world, whom he does not even know nor has seen. Not superficial praying, but intense praying, with tears and lamentations, imploring heaven for the care, comfort, healing, and deliverance for those who are broken and without hope. What grace! What a blessing! What a help! What a comfort! What glories of glories! What supernatural presence and ministry can we experience from the Lord through His sweet Holy Spirit in our time of suffering, when we give ourselves continually to the ministering of others, through the ministry of prayer! No wonder Jesus taught His disciples to pray, "Thy kingdom come, Thy will be done on earth as it is in heaven." **(Matthew 6:10)**

INTERCESSORY PRAYER SHOULD BE MADE FOR RULERS AND LEADERS

As we pray for the world, here's how we could be more specific. We are admonished to pray, *"For kings, and for all that are in authority..."* **(1 Timothy 2:2)** When we pray for those in authority, presidents, prime ministers, governors, mayors, judges, and police officers, especially in our own time of suffering, this will rekindle and ignite revival fires within the spirit.

This also will be a source of comfort as we go through our own trials of affliction. When Joseph sought God in His trials, it affected Egypt. When Daniel sought God in his trials, it affected Babylon. When Samuel sought God in his trials, it affected Israel. And when you seek God through the ministry of prayer for those in authority, it will affect your country as well **(Genesis 41:1-39; Daniel 2:1-48; 1 Samuel 3:1-21; 2 Chronicles 7:14)**. God's people, through prayer, can affect history and change the world. This leads to a quiet, peaceable, godly, and honest life.

Let me take a moment and show you what a catastrophic failure it is when we fail to minister to our nation through the ministry of prayer. When we pray for others and, in this case, our nation, our thoughts are focused, continually remembering the grave responsibility and duty we have been given from God to help maintain and secure the spiritual strength, welfare, and wholesomeness of our country.

The following is an exegesis as to where we are in history, right now, as a nation: *"The wicked shall be turned into hell, and all the nations that forget God."* **(Psalms 9:17)** In this verse, who is God labeling as the wicked? The wicked are directly connected to those who *"forget God." "For I have kept the ways of the LORD, and have not wickedly departed from my God."* **(Psalms 18:21)** According to this verse, to depart from God is the sin of wickedness!

Psalms 18:21 helps to define the "wicked" in **Psalms 9:17**. The wicked are those who do not keep the ways of the Lord: prayer, belief, love and respect for God's Word, and a life which reflects the nature of Christ. In **Psalms 9:17**, the verse is not talking about ungodly forsakers, but godly forgetters. "My people are destroyed for lack of knowledge: because thou hast rejected knowledge, I will also reject thee, that thou shalt be no priest to me: seeing thou hast forgotten the law of thy God, I will also forget thy children." **(Hosea 4:6)** Beloved, our country and nation is in a deplorable state of spiritual apostasy, moral degeneration, and political anarchy. This is not the case because of ungodly forsakers, but because of godly forgetters. Therefore, our country is subjected to and not exempt from the judgment of God...being "turned into hell"–judged of Him!

The church and every believer must pray for the country and the city in which they live. "When it goeth will with the righteous, the city rejoiceth: and when the wicked perish, there is shouting." **(Proverbs 11:10)** The wicked are defeated and the city is rejoicing, because the righteous are praying and doing God's will. "By the blessing of the upright the city is exalted: but it is overthrown by the mouth of the wicked." **(Proverbs 11:11)** How do the upright cause a city to be exalted? Through the blessing of prayer! God admonishes by saying, "Blessed is the nation whose God is the LORD; and the people whom he hath chosen for his own inheritance." **(Psalms 33:12)**. A nation whose God is the Lord is a praying nation! A city exalted is a praying city! A city rejoicing is a praying city! A city, state, or nation which forgets God will practice wickedness, and forgetting God begins with failing to pray! "Righteousness exalteth a nation: but sin is a reproach to any people." **(Proverbs 14:34)** The righteous have a prevailing, overcoming, conquering power that will alter, change, influence and effect change. This weapon that will shake the planet is the almighty bomb called prayer!

As you pray for people whom you know, or may not know, this act of praying will develop within you a genuine care and concern for that person or persons. I've been asked to pray for people many times, who I don't know at all, and as I pray, an intimacy grows within my heart towards the subjects for whom I am praying. When prayer is offered for rulers, it can change the government's course and agenda. I am giving to you now (and in our previous point) a very big picture of prayer. I want you to understand the scope, magnitude, and influence of our praying.

The above verse shows how important it really is to pray for those who are in authority. When we do not universally pray and seek to minister to those who are in authority, it has a corrosive effect upon the entire nation. Many in our nation who profess to be Chirstians do so in name only but not in deed. The candlestick of ministry has been blown out in many churches because of the pursuit of self and the results are devastating! Jesus told the Ephesian church in the book of Revelation, that He had somewhat against them because they had left their first love **(Revelation 2:4)**. The whole message to the Ephesian church, was for the purpose to get them back to the place where they would love God first and more than anything else in the world. How can we know when we have lost our first love for Jesus Christ?

1. *When the emotion of love for Christ no longer supersedes the attractions of the world.*
2. *When the motive and objective of either monetary gain or public recognition supersedes the desire to edify and serve others for the glory of God.*
3. *When prayers are no longer filled with praise, love, affection, and gratitude, but rather with the inquiries of self-consideration.*
4. *When raw excitement and desire slips into ceremonial observances.*
5. *When the processes of thought are more consumed with worldly pleasures and affection rather than Christ.*
6. *When the hunger, thirst, and enthusiasm to search God's Word erodes into a formalistic practice. Instead of being received and believed as a love letter from the Father, through the fellowship of the Holy Spirit, Bible study loses the earnest anticipation to hear our Lord's heart so we can grow closer to Him.*

Use these six essentials to take your own spiritual temperature. Suffering can get us to the place where we pause for a moment and look within and consider this thought: "In what state is my spiritual condition?" Plunging ourselves into all these prayer needs we have considered in this chapter will greatly help to begin the process of emotional, mental healing, and strengthening of the mind, as well as comforts for the soul. When we focus on the needs of others, the preoccupation with our own suffering begins to diminish greatly in our thinking.

A Personal Testimony

One of the greatest men I've ever known taught me personally about the effectiveness and power of prayer. He taught me that prayer moves heaven and influences earth! The man's name was H.L. Woodby, an evangelist.

Brother Woodby came to a small church and listened to me preach one evening. I noticed, as he sat on the front row, that his head mainly was in a bowed, reverential position, and his face was covered with tears and glowed as he prayed during the entire service. After the meeting, Evangelist Woodby approached me and made me to feel like I was the greatest preacher on the planet. What encouragement and care he showed to a very young and inexperienced evangelist.

I'll never forget when he looked at me and out of nowhere said, "If you would allow me, I would love to travel with you everywhere and just pray for you. I see the power and the anointing of God on your ministry and feel that I can be a blessing to it, through the ministry of prayer." Upon hearing those words, I was overcome with much amazement and humility, that he would think such a thing of me.

I responded by saying, "Brother Woodby, I'm not worthy to tie your shoes. If you would be pleased to travel with me, I would love it, but let me please sit at your feet and learn." At that moment a great friendship and a glorious partnership in ministry was born.

In meeting after meeting, state after state, city after city, town after town, I witnessed the miraculous and the spectacular because of the ministry of prayer of this "giant of the faith." I saw the sick healed, churches truly revived, and multitudes of people come to Christ, not as a result of my preaching, but as the result of his praying. I recall, many times, while riding in the car or sleeping in the same room with the great evangelist, when all of a sudden, I would hear moans and weeping, which would turn into lamentations. As I turned my head to see, I looked upon the glorious sight of a man completely consumed by prayer. His arms would be waving toward heaven. His body would be shaking, quivering, and his tears would be flowing as he cried out to heaven for favor and the anointing of God. Much of what I know about prayer, I learned from my friend and mentor, the late evangelist H.L. Woodby.

Conclusion of Praying through Suffering

God cannot do much, if we do not pray much.

God cannot be diligent in our lives, if we are not diligent in prayer.

God only responds to the burden and cries of our heart in prayer.

Prayer keeps us in tune with heaven. When we pray in faith, and our life is consumed with much prayer, God has no choice but to bless and give His power. When we pray, we enter into God's eternal and everlasting realm. This realm is where our affection, desire, and hope should lie. When we continually abide in His sanctuary of prayer, it is then that the material, tangible, and natural world, in which we live, filled with circumstances and challenges, will take on real purpose and meaning in our lives.

"Much of what I could have from You, I do not possess. Much of what You want to do for me, I prevent and limit. The wonder of Your power, the supernatural experience of Your presence, and the blessing of Your peace and comfort I forfeit! All of this I tragically miss, because I fail to pray."

CHAPTER 15

The secret of suffering is found in

THE REVELATION OF GOD

"In the darkest hours of life, it is then Christ is most revealed."

The truth taught in this chapter is the essence and the theme of this entire book. Every topic, theme, and principle taught prior to this chapter and hereafter, finds its fulfillment and accomplished end in the illumination of God Himself. The suffering saint, through persevering faith, presents himself or herself before the Lord helpless, hopeless, and completely given over to Him, upon the altar of uncontested trust.

Our first example is the prophet Isaiah. Isaiah was a mighty prophet to the southern kingdom of Judah. He was a statesman and a scholar: a "polished shaft" for the honor and glory of God. He understood intimately the volatile time in which he lived. His prophecies and messages were not only relevant for his contemporary era, but also were far-reaching into the future.

The topics of his prophecies dealt with the future judgments of his own people (Judah and Jerusalem) if they would not repent and return to God **(Isaiah 1:7-8)**, as well as the coming of the Messiah, first to give His life for the sins and salvation of the world, and second to establish God's earthly millennial kingdom **(Isaiah 53; Isaiah 9:6-7)**.

Isaiah predicts the virgin birth of Christ **(Isaiah 7:14)**. The prophet explains to us how Lucifer fell and became Satan, the perpetual enemy of God **(Isaiah 14:12-14)**. He also predicts in his prophecy, the judgment of the seven-year tribulation period, and of the complete annihilation of every nation, which has come against the people of God, Israel **(Isaiah 24:1-6; 17:12-14)**. In the following passage, Isaiah is going to teach us what he had learned in his time of great suffering and sorrow:

> *In the year that King Uzziah died I saw also the Lord sit-ting upon a throne, high and lifted up, and his train filled the temple. Above it stood the seraphims: each one had six wings; and with twain he covered his feet and with twain he did fly. And one cried unto another, and said, Holy, holy, holy, is the Lord of hosts: the whole earth is full of his glory. And the posts of the door moved at the voice of him that cried, and the house was filled with smoke. Then said I, Woe is me! for I am undone; because I am a man of unclean lips, and I dwell in the midst of a people of unclean lips: for mine eyes have seen the King, the Lord of hosts. Then flew one of the sera-phims unto me, having a live coal in his hand, which he had taken with the tongs from off the altar: and he laid it upon my mouth, and said, Lo, this hath touched thy lips; and thine iniquity is taken away, and thy sin purged. Also I heard the voice of the Lord, saying, Whom shall I send, and who will go for us? Then said I, Here am I; send me.*
>
> (ISAIAH 6:1-8)

The godly and good King Uzziah had died. For fifty-two years under his reign, the southern kingdom of Judah had prospered. They were victori-ous in battle, grew industrially, and for the most part, it was a time of peace and safety for the people of God. In his last days, the king became filled with pride, ego, and arrogance. The king unlawfully went into the temple to perform duties that only the priest under the Mosaic Law had the com-mission to fulfill. When reproved by the priests for his sacrilegious actions, he became angry and furious instead of humbly repenting. As a result of this, God struck the disobedient King with leprosy, which finally led to his destruction and untimely death **(2 Chronicles 27:16-21)**.

Upon Uzziah's death, his son Jotham succeeded his father, becoming king. Jotham did not have the character or the skills of his father. The threat of warfare from the north, like dim beating drums, was now a cause for alarm and anxiety. It was under these conditions of fear and uncertainty that Isaiah fled into the temple to seek the face of God.

God revealed Himself in majestic splendor, giving to His quaking, fearful son internal strength through the magnificence of this vision, the outward show of the Almighty's force! God was showing His servant Isaiah, that the earthly king was corruptible, which was manifested in the outward plight of his leprosy, but the King of Kings is the incorruptible God, the eternal King, which can never be corrupted, tainted, defiled, or lose His potency. His is a throne which can never be overtaken by an enemy, a throne that is higher and mightier than any frail throne of man, worldly military campaign, or spiritual enemy that would try to come against us. For He is the Lord of Hosts!

What confidence can this bring, when our inward eye of faith super-naturally sees the vision of the incorruptible God, who sits far above the corruption of anything this world can put before us. This can transform our fearful heart into a fearless heart, which can completely rest with consolation and surety in the thrice holy God, who occupies His throne.

When loss invades our life, whether it be of possessions, health, or loved ones, we can begin to see more clearly treasures of the soul greater than anything this life could possibly hope to offer. After the richest summer, when the trees are in full bloom, blanketing mountain tops and fields like a beautifully woven bedspread, the fall creeps in, starving the mighty trees of their chlorophyll and changing the artistic tapestry from a deep green pomp into an amalgamation of splendid color. Bright leaves quickly fade, shrivel up and fall to the ground, leaving the woods naked, allowing the eyes to see in full view vast landscapes, which before were hidden behind the veil of thick foliage.

When God allows our physical and carnal distractions to fade away, we can then see more clearly God's eternal purpose, will, and plan for our life. We can also enter into a sanctuary of close intimacies with the King of heaven. When we suffer, we become more sensitive and open to ideas and thoughts that perhaps were never entertained prior to our suffering. It is in these times that God can extend our faith beyond the usual or ordinary and help us to see things in size and scope that we could never see before.

Consider the details of Isaiah's vision as set before us here in this passage. "Above the throne of God stood the angelic choir of seraphims, each having six wings. With two of their wings they covered their face, with two of their wings they covered their feet, and two of their wings they did fly." What did all this mean to the suffering and struggling Isaiah? The wings covering the face of these angelic creatures shows their humility, submission, and reverence before God.

I guarantee you, after Isaiah left the temple, his life greatly deepened in these characteristics. "With two wings they covered their feet." This shows their sanctification (separated for the purposes of God only) and commitment to holiness in all they say and do. Bless the Lord, God of heaven! I believe the greatest resulting outcome of personal suffering is to strive after a holier life.

"Also, with two wings they did fly." This shows the readiness to serve, a willing obedience to act upon the commands of God. In continual motion and activity, every movement and full expression of these angelic beings was consumed to bring honor and glory to their Lord. Isaiah would learn that in the darkest of hours, as storm clouds would hover overhead, God would be glorified. The Lord's purposes would be fulfilled, and His servants would be the active agents, who would look to Him and bring Him glory even when peril and loss struck their lives! These **seraphims** are a beautiful picture of self-effacement, sanctification, and eager anticipated servitude. These things should control and motivate our lives as well.

Isaiah also saw, in this illustrious vision, the long flowing garments of the sovereign God that filled the temple. This is a symbol of omnipotence (God having all power and authority over all things.) None of our conflicts of life or the source of these conflicts have control over our circumstances, whether it be a spouse, parent, child, co-worker, church member, government authority, civil authority, business adversity or illness. This power belongs to the one who has final and full authority over all the matters and issues of life and death. God is the one whose train fills the temple.

Isaiah was enveloped, surrounded, and overwhelmed with the smoke of God, which filled the house. This smoke is symbolic of the presence of God, in the person of the Holy Spirit, the third person of the Trinity. Isaiah could not have felt safer than in this solemn moment. Think of yourself right in the middle of a thick fog. You can't see anything, but the cloud which overshadows you. In any direction you look, the sight is nothing but a deep mass of mist, which yields no visibility and can even cause disorientation. All you can do in a moment like that is be still, and with every movement exercise extreme caution. In the midst of your trials, God desires to completely enclose and enfold you with His covering. "Be still and know that I am God..." **(Psalms 46:10)** He wants you to be overcome by His presence and not circumstances.

Instead of fear, doubt, and worry encircling you, the Holy Spirit would rather clothe you in His glory, great beauty, grandeur, magnificence with the knowledge that He is present. He will surround you with confidence and comfort, and cause you to see only the invisible God, and not your physical circumstances. Therefore a legion of fears, standing without, will never be able to pierce through the thick smoke that has you nestled within the fortified walls of His temple. The prophet was no doubt awestruck with inward assurance and confidence as he felt the whole temple shake and move at the voice of the angelic creature. This voice yielded a message of hope and deliverance. When God arrives on the scene, it is accompanied by a demonstrative movement. In your case, it will not be within the walls of the temple, but rather within the house of your soul. This is where God will give you the vision of His glory and yield to you the sweet peaceable effects of His sovereign rule over all the worries that would attempt to control your heart.

God used this trial of affliction in Isaiah's life to drive him into the temple to seek God. While in that secret place with the Lord, God was able to reveal many truths to His servant. Isaiah realized he was a part of the problem, and God would use him as a part of the solution. It was in this moment of suffering, that Isaiah received his call and commission from the Lord. As he saw the holiness of God, he had an acute awareness of his own exceeding sinfulness and failures. God did not condemn him, but rather cleansed him and prepared him for the Master's use. Isaiah's suffering allowed him to see more clearly. He saw and experienced the following:

- He realized his own shortcoming and responsibility.
- Outward circumstances do not control the counsels of God.
- An eternal perspective must be embraced beyond any event which occurs in the natural.
- Holiness is the most desired purpose God has for His children.
- God is God alone, occupying His everlasting throne of covenant-blessing and fulfilled promise.
- God offers merciful cleansing and forgiveness.
- God provides comfort and confidence in times of trouble and need.
- Everything in the natural and supernatural realm is subjected to God's rule and authority.

Isaiah saw some things, understood some things, experienced some things, heard and realized some things that he would've never seen, understood, experienced, heard, or realized had God not allowed him to go through his time of suffering.

Consider Moses and his life experience. Moses suffered the loss of every worldly pleasure and dignity, *"Choosing rather to suffer affliction with the people of God..."* **(Hebrews 11:25)** He gave up power, wealth, fame, self-gratification, and an earthly throne to enter into a sanctuary of life that would allow him to behold and enjoy experiences from an invisible God, which became magnificently visible through his suffering. This suffering and affliction speaks of severe persecution and ill-treatment.

Like the nation of Israel, in our time of suffering, God knows exactly where we are. "And the LORD said, I have surely seen the affliction of my people which are in Egypt, and have heard their cries by reason of their taskmasters; for I know their sorrows." **(Exodus 3:7)** *God* reassured Moses that He was neither blind nor ambivalent to the needs and struggles of His people. He saw their afflictions, heard their cries, knew their sorrows, and came to where they were.

Likewise, God does the same thing for you. Not only did God make it clear that He knew of their desperate condition, He also made it clear that His deliverance, on their behalf, would be complete. "And I am come down to deliver them out of the hand of the Egyptians, and to bring them up out of that land onto a good land and a large, unto a land flowing with milk and honey..." **(Exodus 3:8a)** Out of the bitter bondage of slavery, God enabled Moses and the nation of Israel to experience Him in a unique union, with an outward show of His mighty works. What was the process which God employed? What was the experience of Moses, the nation of Israel, and even of Pharaoh and the Egyptians?

First, God would not do anything until Moses, by choice, forfeited the grandeur and pleasures of Egypt. God revealed Himself to Moses, causing him to see God's wondrous appearance and hear His voice out of the burning bush on top of the mountain of God at Horeb **(Exodus 3:1-5)**. At this meeting, God instructed Moses to go back to Egypt and deliver His people out of their miseries and bitter sufferings. Isn't it amazing, Moses could not deliver anyone out of their sufferings until he first learned how to successfully endure, through his own sufferings, with the help of God? Moses received his training from the Lord as he struggled and endured on the backside of the desert for forty years. Suffering is never for us alone, but always for blessing of others. An entire nation of believers and unbelievers was able to witness the spectacle of an Almighty God as He pounded His enemy (Pharaoh and Egypt) with ten miraculous and undeniable plagues, which were issued from His throne of mercy and judgment.

What did the suffering saints of God witness in that day? They saw water turned to blood; plagues of frogs, lice, flies, and diseased cattle; an outbreak of boils upon man and beasts; a fiery hailstorm; a plague of locusts; pervasive darkness; and the death of every firstborn Egyptian.

Moses was one-on-one with God when the Lord gave to him the law **(Exodus 19:11-24).** Moses again met with God on the top of Mount Sinai **(Exodus 24:12-18)**. God personally talked with Moses as he entered the tabernacle, "And the LORD spake unto Moses face-to-face, as a man speaketh onto his friend." **(Exodus 33:11)** Moses also requested of the Lord, that he might see the face of God in the fullness of His glory, not to see God's face, and the form of his body, apart from the fullness of His glory, as he had experienced in the past **(Exodus 16:10; 24:16-17; 33:18-23)**. God explained to Moses his request was not possible, but the Lord would hide him in the cleft of a rock, and as the Lord passed by, He would cover Moses with His hand and then, would allow him to look at the fullness of His glory from behind!

My mind is going wild at this thought: How safe, secure, and fortified Moses must have felt in that moment, being surrounded by the hard rock of the mountain, then canopied by the hand of God. As God passed by, Moses saw the might, protection, and tenderness of God's hand. Then from behind, Moses was able to witness and see the one who fills the universe and eternity **(Isaiah 57:15)**. The only person outside of Moses to see God so intimately and personally is the second person of the Trinity Himself, the Son of God, the Lord Jesus **(John 1:18)**.

Moses and the nation of Israel saw some things, understood some things, experienced some things, heard and realized some things that they would've never seen, understood, experienced, heard, or realized, had God not allowed them to go through their time of suffering.

Shadrach, Meshach, and Abednego were cast into King Nebuchadnezzar's raging, fiery furnace because they would not bow down to and worship this wicked king's marvelous idol of gold. This image of gold stood 125 feet high and was being used by the king to unify all the people under his rule. This was an attempt to subject the entire kingdom to a "one world" religion, which had as its head, the king himself. Shadrach, Meshach, and Abednego's refusal to compromise, would cost them their very life.

After being arrested, they were brought into the presence of the king. The king harshly put them on trial and examined their decision, as to why they would defy the king's decree. These three young men made a strong declaration of their faith, love, and loyalty to the one true God. Their conviction was steadfast and unwavering.

The king, in an uncontrolled rampage, ordered his servants to make his furnace seven times hotter than normal. The smoke and the fire violently billowed out of the mouth of the furnace. Fully clothed, Shadrach, Meshach, and Abednego were bound securely and thrust into the bowels of the flames. The furnace was so hot, it immediately killed the strong, powerful gladiators who hurled these boys into this deathtrap.

With great astonishment and bewilderment, as the king peered down into his instrument of execution, he saw a supernatural, miraculous event unfolding before his very eyes. A fourth person was walking among the three Hebrew youths. This fourth person was identified by the king himself: "Did not we cast three men bound into the midst of the fire?" His servants answered and said, "True, O King." Notice the response of the King. "He answered and said, Lo, I see four men loose, walking in the midst of the fire, and they have no hurt; and the form of the fourth is like the Son of God." **(Daniel 3:24b-25)** God allowed King Nebuchadnezzar to recognize the second person of the Trinity.

In a time of suffering and terror, these three young men experienced intimacy with God. Were there any words exchanged between them as they walked in the midst of the fire together? I am sure they saw that they had made God proud through their willingness to give their lives for Him. There is a great treasure of truth here for all who are going through their own personal "fiery furnace" of suffering. These three Hebrew young men had an assured hope beyond the natural flames of the fire, which might have consumed them. They did not focus on the flames, but on their Heavenly Father. They were able to look past the worldly king, who tried to intimidate and oppress them, and see by faith the King of Kings, who gave them strength, wisdom, and a will to persevere.

Listen to their confidence. *"If it be so, our God whom we serve is able to deliver us from the burning fiery furnace, and he will deliver us out of thine hand, O King. But if not, be it known unto thee, O King, that we will not serve thy gods, nor worship the golden image which thou hast set up."* **(Daniel 3:17-18)** The emphatic fact we learn here is that God will always deliver us. Finally and ultimately, we will always be victorious and triumphant in all of our trials. These boys were resting in a glorious principle taught in the New Testament: *"So when this corruptible* (our bodies which might be burned up in these fires) *shall have put on incorruption, and this mortal* (our temporary life) *shall have put on immortality, then shall be brought to pass the saying that is written, death is swallowed up in victory. O death, where is thy sting? Ò grave, where is thy victory? The sting of death is sin; and the strength of sin is the law. But thanks be to God, which giveth us the victory through our Lord Jesus Christ."* **(1 Corinthians 15:54-57)** At the bottom of the furnace, they continued walking. Why? Because they had a path and course, and a finish line at which to arrive **(2 Timothy 4:7)**.

They knew their final destination would not be the flames of that pit, but the fullness of joy in the Father's house. The psalmist put it this way: *"Yea, though I walk through the valley of the shadow of death, I will fear no evil: for thou art with me..."* **(Psalms 23:4)** These young men were in the flames and shadow of death, yet they were not alone. God was with them. Multitudes of Babylon's citizens witnessed the spectacle of God's great deliverance of the servants of the Lord. Shadrach, Meshach, and Abednego brought glory and honor to God through their time of extreme suffering **(Daniel 3:28-29)**. The only thing missing and destroyed when these three young men came out of the fire were the cords which did bind them. This I believe is one of the main results of suffering: we become free in those areas of life that kept us in bondage.

Shadrach, Meshach, and Abednego saw some things, understood some things, experienced some things, heard and realized some things that they would've never seen, understood, experienced, heard, or realized had God not allowed them to go through their time of suffering.

140

Likewise, Daniel the prophet had a similar experience to that of Shadrach, Meshach, and Abednego. Under the Medo-Persian King Darius, Daniel was hurled into the jaws of death. He was thrown into a den of ravenous, bloodthirsty lions. These brutes of the wild were killing machines. They were purposely starved for this type of execution, wherein the accused criminal would be mercilessly slaughtered and consumed by these jungle beasts. Daniel held the highest office of leadership within the kingdom, second only to the king himself. Daniel was very loved and respected by the king, but he was hated and despised by all others who held a place of authority within the king's administration.

As a result of their disdain for Daniel, they conspired together to entrap him and make him look like a traitor to the king. With much intrigue they developed their plot and presented it before the king. Because of his arrogance, the King Darius fell for the scheme and signed a decree that no person could ask a petition of any god or man for thirty days except of the king only. Even though Daniel knew this law was put into place temporarily, he opened his window and knelt towards Jerusalem three times a day and prayed, making supplication before his God. Of course you know what all the conspirators did; they ran to the king and ratted out Daniel. The king's heart was very sad. Having no choice, he allowed Daniel to be cast into the den of lions **(Daniel 6:14-16)**.

Something incredible and extraordinary happened within that dark, cold pit of despair. God sent an angel of the Lord to protect Daniel. I believe with all of my heart the angel which God sent was *"the lion of the tribe of Judah."* **(Revelation 5:5)** The Lord Jesus Christ Himself appeared in the fullness of His glory. God's lion (Christ) stood between Daniel and those vicious hunters, and with a loud cacophonous roar, quenched their boisterous growls, causing them to quickly retreat in docile submission!

Can you imagine spending a whole night with the angel of God? What were the conversations between this angel and Daniel? Perhaps that evening God revealed to Daniel the many prophecies recorded in the book which bears his name. If I were Daniel, I would not have taken my eyes off that angel for a moment. Maybe the angel told Daniel to rest and sleep, assuring him that He would keep a safe watch until the morning. There is no doubt Daniel experienced the complete peace of God as he passed the night with the hostile company of carnivores. Yet, he was fortified within the stronghold of that heavenly visitor.

King Darius had no peace. He passed the night troubled and conflicted as he worried about his most loyal subject within that dungeon of doom **(Daniel 6:18)**. Early the next morning, the king ran with haste to the den of lions and with anxious excitement yelled out to Daniel to inquire what had become of him. His inquiry was remarkable: "...O Daniel, servant of the living God, is thy God, whom thou servest continually, able to deliver thee from the lions?" Daniel's response brought great delight and comfort to the King's soul. "....O king, live forever. My God hath sent his angel, and hath shut the lions' mouths that they have not hurt me: forasmuch as before him innocency was found in me..." **(Daniel 6:20-22)**

After eighty years of faithful service, Daniel had done the right thing by putting his Lord first before all others. It must be understood that this den of lions was a cold, damp, dark place of terror! A massive stone was laid upon the mouth of this pit to completely seal in the condemned prisoner. The ghastly stench of death seasoned the bitter air of that tomb as the remainder of the corpses of those formerly slain emanated foul odors throughout the atmosphere of that tightly sealed lair. Then suddenly, the day Dawn and the Day Star shined brilliantly into the blackness of that place, blinding the wild savages and dispelling the darkness with illuminating light, while providing warmth and comfort for the saint of God.

All Daniel knew from his youth was pain, suffering, and heartbreak. He witnessed the violent Babylonian army completely besiege and crush the city of his home. He probably watched the horrors of his people, even his own immediate family members, being executed before his very eyes. He was ripped away from his family, enslaved by a strange people, and marched many miles away into a strange land, and was now all alone, oppressed by the enemy. He did not stagger in his faith. He was unwavering in his love and devotion toward the Heavenly Father. He was able, by God's grace, to keep himself from bitterness toward his captors. As a result of his pursuit of God, Daniel was able to overcome every tragic event that would attack his mind, body, and soul.

I'm telling you my friend Daniel saw some things, understood some things, experienced some things, and heard some things, that otherwise he would have never seen, understood, experienced, or heard, had God not allowed him to go through his time of suffering.

Stephen, another servant of God, in his moment of severe suffering experienced the presence of God, allowing him to see and touch the other side. While preaching the gospel of Jesus Christ to a large group of false-religionists, comprised of different sects from the synagogue, along with the elders and many other Jewish attendees, Stephen experienced a remarkable revelation from God. Before we jump right into the middle of this astounding event, the groundwork must be laid as to why such an experience could even be made possible for Stephen. Back in chapter three of this book, it was stated that we have already been delivered, because of Calvary. Now comes the second major theme of this book and it is apropos that we insert it here.

We have been delivered because of the Comforter

The **Comforter** is the Spirit of God. Stephen was filled with the Holy Ghost and faith **(Acts 6:5, 8)**. His message was electrifying, informative, compelling, and very convicting! His preaching was heart arresting and moving.

Stephen started his message by going all the way back and explaining the call of Abraham. Then he taught the people that God gave to Abraham covenants and promises. He shared the story of Joseph and then explained how the people of Israel became bound in slavery by the Egyptians. He went on to teach extensively about the life of Moses, how Moses spent the first forty years of his life receiving an education by the Egyptians. Stephen also explained how Moses, being refused and rejected by his own people, fled Egypt. Then, this brilliant, bold preacher taught his anxious listeners that for the next forty years, Moses received divine training by God, finally to be rejected and rebelled against by the people of Israel during the last forty years of his life. The final two points of Stephen's message were the hard facts that God's people remained in rebellion and in defiance of His Word, the prophets, and of His Christ to that very day **(Genesis 12:1-9; 13:14-18; 15:1-21; 17:6-19; 22:15-18; 37:28-34; 41:1 - 50:26; Exodus 1:7-22; 2:10 - 4:31; 5:1 - 19:2; 32:1-6; Numbers 12-14; Judges 2:11-14; Amos 5:25-27; Acts 57:51-53)**.

Stephen's audience vehemently rejected the Word of Truth given to them. They became rabidly violent and out of control. This mob of religious leaders and common people, both men and women, surrounded Stephen with the intent to murder him, and he knew it.

What happened next was astonishing. Luke, a physician and the writer of the book of Acts, gives us a detailed narrative of this phenomenal event. Stephen, in the midst of his suffering and persecution, "…looked up steadfastly into heaven, and saw the glory of God, and Jesus standing on the right hand of God, And said, Behold, I see the heavens opened, and the Son of man standing on the right hand of God." **(Acts 7:54-56)** The crowd, in the state of their deranged and frenzied anarchy, maliciously dragged him outside of the city and stoned him mercilessly.

As the stones were bludgeoning his body and crushing his skull, out of the shriek and cacophony of that deranged God-hating and Christ-rejecting crowd, Stephen, called upon God. In that moment, as the congregation in one accord viciously assaulted this saint of God, Stephen did not act out of anger in return for their cruel violation of him. He did not shout back at them with cursing and insults as a result of their evil aggression towards him. No, the contrary is so. He repaid their hostility and ill-treatment with love, mercy, grace, and a prayer to God for their forgiveness, *"And they stoned Stephen, calling upon God, and saying, Lord Jesus, receive my spirit. And he kneeled down, and cried with a loud voice, Lord, lay not this sin to their charge. And when he had said this, he fell asleep."* (Acts 7:59-60)

Stephen, in his moment of severe suffering, was able to see some things, hear some things, experience some things, know some things,

and understand some things, that otherwise he would've never been able to see, hear, experience, know or understand, had God not allowed him to go through his time of suffering.

How was Stephen able to persevere, forbear, and endure during this horrific event? Consider the following:

- Stephen was filled with the Word of God. This is the reason I gave the many Old Testament references, which Stephen pulled from, as he preached his mighty sermon.
- Stephen was full of faith and of the Holy Ghost **(Acts 6:5; 7:55)**.
- Stephen humbled himself before God and man, keeping himself from bitterness **(Acts 7:60)**.
- In his time of trouble, he did not look anywhere else, but up to God **(Acts 7:55)**.
- As a result of being skilled in the Scriptures, he was able to apply the wisdom of God to his situation.
- Because of his diligent approach to the Word of God, the filling of the Holy Spirit, and his unshakable faith, he was granted great power **(Acts 6:8)**.
- He spent so much time with God, it was manifested and evidenced upon his entire countenance **(Acts 6:15)**.
- While Stephen was enveloped in the rain of rocks, he completely immersed and enveloped himself in prayer **(Acts 7:59)**.

The most important part of this story concerning Stephen, is the truth that he was filled with the Holy Spirit of God. The Holy Spirit cannot be described as an "it" or a thing, but rather He is a real person. He is the third person of the Holy Trinity, co-equal, co-eternal, and co-existing with the Heavenly Father and the Lord Jesus Christ. As a person, He can be grieved (which means he can feel pain) **(Ephesians 4:30)**. He can be quenched or ignored **(1 Thessalonians 5:19)**. The Holy Spirit is the faithful witness who lives within our soul and will abide with us forever **(John 14:26; Romans 8:16)**. In the story of Stephen, we find the entire Godhead actively engaged and involved with everything going on with him. He was, *"...full of the Holy Ghost...and saw... Jesus standing on the right hand of God."* (Acts 7:55-56)

At the same time that Stephen was surrounded by his problems, he was also surrounded by the "three in one" God. His God, Lord, Savior, and ever present help (the Holy Spirit) stood with him during the perilous encounter. The same is true when we suffer: we are never alone. When Jesus taught His disciples that He would be sending the gift of His Holy Spirit, He explained to them that He had asked His Heavenly Father to send them another Comforter.

Stop and think about this for a moment: in His earthly ministry Jesus was physically with His disciples. While in His presence, the disciples never experienced fear or anxiety. How can one be scared or afraid when the very person of God is with them? When Jesus went back to His Heavenly Father—this is known as the ascension of Christ—He shortly thereafter, sent the gift which He had promised, His indwelling presence, the person of the Holy Spirit. In our Lord's earthly ministry and prior to His ascension, Jesus would prepare His disciples for the severe conflicts which would lie ahead. All of the apostles of Christ would experience hardship and suffering in their very near future. Such is the case here with Stephen, who was not among the twelve, but he was one of God's chosen and more than that...a child of God.

These truths apply to all of God's people down through the ages, right up to the 21st century. The teaching of our Lord on the subject is so clear. He said to His disciples twelve hours before His arrest, *"Even the Spirit of truth; whom the world cannot receive, because it seeth him not, neither knoweth him: but ye know him; for he dwellest with you"* presently, right now, because I am here, *"and shall be in you."* Jesus went on to say, *"I will not leave you comfortless: I will come to you"* in the future because I will come back and live in your heart (John 14:17-18).

What a blanket of covering. Can God get any closer than being right inside of you? Often children will sleep with stuffed animals, or with a light on, to keep them safe and secure throughout the night. God's little children, however, in their waking and sleeping moments always have with them the eternal God, a loving Heavenly Father, the parent of all parents, the protector of all protectors, the guide of all guides, the caregiver of all caregivers, the comforter of all comforters, and the helper of all helpers!

Jesus called the Holy Spirit the "Comforter." The Greek word for comforter is *"Parakletos,"* which means, one called to the side of another for help or counsel. The Holy Ghost is our *"Parakletos"* on earth, and our resurrected Lord Jesus is our *"Parakletos"* in heaven. Sometimes our suffering is so severe, we cannot even understand or interpret our own emotions. Agonies that run so deep can perplex the soul and confuse the mind. The Spirit of God can go to the place where no psychologist, psychiatrist, or counselor can reach. He can move into our intellect and bring a sense of calm and quietness where reason and logic would attempt to wreak havoc. He can operate within the soul and replace fear and anxiety with peace and comfort. He can penetrate and remove every thought of doubt, and in its stead, place confidence and assurance.

This is what the psalmist meant when he prayed, "O LORD, thou hast searched me, and known me. Thou knowest my downsitting and mine uprising, thou understandest my thought afar off. Thou compassest my path and my lying down, and art acquainted with all my ways. For there is not a word in my tongue, but, lo, O LORD, thou knowest it altogether. Thou hast beset me behind and before, and laid thy hand upon me. Search me, O God, and know my heart: try me, and know my thoughts." **(Psalms 139:1-5; 23)**

These verses describe a depth of intimacy and knowing on the part of our Lord as it relates to everything we go through in times of our suffering and every other aspect of our life as well. As we diligently pursue and look to God in our seemingly impossible challenges, every mental and moral conflict, weakness and flaw will be subjugated and overpowered by the Spirit of God! Furthermore, He can take all of our inarticulable, damaged emotions and bring them into the very presence of our loving, Great High Priest, Jesus Christ, and plead our cause. This is His work, what He does. *"Likewise the Spirit also helpeth our infirmities: for we know not what we should pray for as we ought: but the Spirit itself maketh intercession for us with groanings which cannot be uttered."* **(Romans 8:26)** The word "infirmities" refer to any maladies of the physical body or the soul.

Every and any emotional or mental conflict can be described as an infirmity. A further description of this word explains, at times, our inability to understand what may be taking place within or around us. The Spirit makes intercession with groaning. His groaning pierces the very heart of the One who sits on the throne. Our helper and ever present friend, the Holy Spirit, conveys to Jesus our Lord, the heartfelt gushing of our every burden, need, emotion, anxiety, stress, fear, and the complexity of our thoughts. In **Hebrews 4:15**, we see that Jesus, who is touched with the feelings of our infirmities, experiences our every burden with us through the ministry of the Holy Spirit. "For we have not an high priest which cannot be touched with the feeling of our infirmities; but was in all points tempted like as we are, yet without sin."

It is interesting to note that the Apostle John in his gospel is the only one who uses the term of "Comforter" to refer directly to the person of the Holy Ghost. This is the perfect place in our study of the subject of suffering to look deeply into the example the Apostle John has left for us. He left us a legacy of hope for in the time of our own suffering.

The Apostle John became known as "the apostle of love" because of this constant theme in his writings. He knew rejection, persecution, and suffering. In the early church era, John, as well as the other apostles, were perceived as a great threat to the political stability of Rome. The Roman Emperor Domitian, along with the emperors before him, were self-proclaimed gods. Because of the constant threats to their thrones which surrounded them daily, these men were driven by paranoid, schizophrenic delusions. Hence, they became great persecutors of the early church. This young Christian religion of the first century converted thousands away from the false-religious systems of that day and the polytheism (the worship of many gods) of the Roman Empire. The Christians wrought many miracles in the name of their king, Jesus. The theme of their message was

Jesus crucified, buried, and risen from the dead, ascended back into glory to one day return and establish His kingdom.

The Apostle John was one of the great church leaders and carried a lot of influence. Sources of early church history, like Tertullian, Jerome, and Foxe, described the attempted execution of the Apostle John by the madman, Roman Emperor, Domitian. Domitian was ruthless, cunning, and brutal. He had Christians impaled and used as human torches to light his garden at night. He had Christians thrown into the Coliseum and ripped apart by wild dogs and lions. These spectacles were public entertainment for the citizens of the Roman Empire.

Furthermore, Christians were sawn asunder and thrown off of high cliffs onto sharp protruding spears below. They were tied up and dragged facedown by wild horses over the rough cobblestones. They were also sewn up into sheepskins and goatskins and made to wander in the deserts, mountains, caves, and dens of the earth **(Hebrews 11:35-38)**. While the Apostle John was pastor of the church of Ephesus, Domitian had him arrested and publicly lowered into a vat of boiling oil in an attempt to kill this radical church leader of great influence, silencing him once and for all. It has been stated by the witnesses of this event, as the Apostle John was lowered into the boiling oil, they heard no screams of a tortured soul. They heard only this great saint of God preaching the love of Jesus Christ and of His gospel which would eternally save all those who would believe.

Through the billowing smoke emanating off the boiling oil, the spectators heard not the wailing of one writhing in pain, but rather one proclaiming the wonderful works of God. The large crowd of witnesses changed. They demanded that John be released, and multitudes were converted to Christ. This failed attempt to execute and to silence the servant of God moved Emperor Domitian to exile John to a small, rocky, treeless, penal island called Patmos. This island was reserved for the lowest of criminals.

John would be silenced now. He would have no more influence, being removed and isolated from any human contact...so the Emperor thought. Listen to the words of the Apostle John, as he writes to the seven churches of Asia, "I John, who also am your brother, and companion in tribulation, and in the kingdom and patience of Jesus Christ, was in the isle that is called Patmos, for the word of God, and for the testimony of Jesus Christ." **(Revelation 1:9)**

John called himself a companion in tribulation, meaning suffering. He knew what it meant to suffer and to persevere in faith. Glory! Glory! Glory! What did God do for John in the midst of all of his suffering? He showed and revealed unto him the entire book of the Revelation of things to come. In chapters one through three, John saw the resurrected glorified Christ in all His splendor and majesty. In chapter four, he saw the very throne of God! This throne was magnificient and glorious, a throne of sovereignty. As Jesus sat on His throne the Apostle John described Him as a jasper and sardine stone. He appeared as a brilliant, glistening diamond with a beautiful deep red presence. Around the throne was an emerald-like rainbow, which illuminated an indescribable color scheme of green. John saw around that sublime throne four unique creatures, each having six mighty wings full of eyes. The first beast was like a lion, and the second beast was like a calf, and the third beast had the face of a man, and the fourth beast was like a flying eagle.

John the Revelator witnessed the spectacle of lightnings, thunderings, seven burning lamps, and voices round about the throne. John noticed the floor of this "throne room" was like a sea of transparent glass. He could look down and its view was marvelous in endless resplendency! John heard the four creatures singing and praising God, revering Him for the most glorious of His moral attributes: *"Holy, holy, holy, Lord God Almighty, which was, and is, and is to come."* At the same time, he saw the twenty-four elders bowed prostrate in adoration before the throne, worshiping!

In chapter five, the Apostle John sees the first person of the Trinity holding a little book in His hand. This little book was the title deed to all the earth and in it disclosing the divine legal right and privilege of only one person who was worthy enough to open the book and loose the seals thereof. John heard and saw an incalculable number of angels praising the Lord Jesus, because He (his Lord and Savior) was worthy to reach out and take from the hand of the Almighty the book and open it to fulfill and complete the eternal purposes and counsel of God. In chapter six, John saw the white horse, red horse, black horse, and the pale horse, along with all their riders sent forth to oppress and conquer.

The Lord showed John that one day He would shake the entire universe as He judged the earth. John witnessed God's future judgement. In his vision he saw God send a great earthquake, make the sun black, turn the moon into blood, and cause the stars to fall from heaven to earth. John saw every mountain and island violently moved out of its place, along with every person on the planet hiding or fleeing from the dread of The Most High God! John saw in chapters seven and eight the 144,000 Jewish evangelists separated to spread the gospel to the entire globe. He saw hail, fire, and blood rain from heaven. He saw a burning meteor fall from the sky and a great star by the name of Wormwood fall from heaven to poison a third part of the waters. Also, he witnessed the third part of the sun moon and stars darkened! In Revelation chapter nine, God revealed one of the most horrific visions to the Apostle John concerning future judgment. God showed John a bottomless pit, out of which were released grotesque-looking locust-like creatures. They were to sting man with their tails and torment them with all the symptoms of death for five months.

Also, an army of two million demons was released to kill a third of all mankind. In this magnificent revelation John beheld God's two "super" witnesses, as well as the unholy trinity of the Antichrist, the false prophet, and the dragon. God, like a motion picture in an IMAX theater, rolled before the apostle the scenes of the Great War in heaven between the devil and Michael and his angels. John was able to see how God one day would judge the military, mercantile, and false-religious systems of the world. At the same time, John understood that God would regather, restore and protect Israel.

During this revelation, John is being persecuted! Cast out! Rejected! He is suffering, all alone, on this barren rock island called Patmos.

Pause for a moment, dear reader. Consider the reality of what is taking place. Right in the midst of John's peril, he understood clearly, through all of his experiences (as did the others referenced in this chapter), that God ministers, sustains, controls, cares and provides for the sufferer in his journey in great detail, throughout the whole process. John's peril would be the equivalency of your hospital stay, your long arduous frightful wait in the doctor's office, your trip into surgery, your lonely days and nights of incarceration, your grieving and mourning over the departure of friends and loved ones through sickness and death, your deep unexplainable depression resulting from the everyday pressures of life, or your laborious perseverance as you provide around-the-clock care for a helpless, impaired loved one.

In his continued experience on this barren, wasteland of an island, John went on to hear the victorious announcements of God's triumph over His enemies and the proclamation that the long-anticipated marriage supper of the Lamb was now ready to begin. God gave John a future vision of the following:

- The epic battle of Armageddon.
- The binding of Satan and his casting down into the bottomless pit for 1,000 years.
- The fulfillment of the many Old Testament prophecies concerning the millennial reign of Christ.
- The last and final universal world war battle of Gog and Magog.
- The undefinable and unparalleled glorious vision of the city of God, the city of gold.
- The glories of the new heaven and earth.

John also witnessed, through a vision, the dreaded last and final judgment of the unsaved dead, known in the Bible as the Great White Throne Judgment. Finally, he heard the sweetest and most wonderful invitation of our Lord and Savior: *"And the Spirit and the bride say, Come. And let him that heareth say, Come. And let him that is athirst come. And whosoever will, let him take the water of life freely."* (Revelation 22:17)

My beloved reader, John saw some things, heard some things, experienced some things, realized some things, and understood

some things, that he would've never seen, heard, experienced, realized, or understood, if God had not allowed him to go through his time of great persecution and rejection.

Persevering in faith as we suffer is the gateway and door of great opportunity to experience God supernaturally, in a way that not even heaven itself could fulfill in our soul.

CHAPTER 16

UNDERSTANDING OUR SUFFERING

IN THE PRESENT

"If we cannot look beyond the physical and tangible, we
will forever be confused and lost in this life."

We've already considered up to this point two prolific truths:

I. **We have been delivered because of Calvary.**

II. **We have been delivered because of the Comforter.**

Now we must come to realize that:

I. **We have been delivered because Christ is coming again!**

How do we view our suffering in the present?
First, we must realize that our trials are <u>appointed</u>.
The Apostle Paul explained to the Thessalonian church the following truth: "That no man should be moved by these afflictions: for yourselves know that we are appointed thereunto." **(1 Thessalonians 3:3)** When we find ourselves in trouble and conflict, God is not taken by surprise. He

knows where we are and He knows what we need. We often want "now" answers for what seems to be an unsolvable equation. God's has an eternal purpose for our lives. Paul realized this. Therefore, he was able to give us the great truth of **Romans 8:28**. The greatest example of this principle I can find in the Bible is the story of Job. It would take another whole book to expound the relationship between God and Job's sufferings, but I want to give you an overview of what Job learned, as he went through his appointed, God-given trial:

- In the heavens, God simultaneously and continually works out His unique purposes for the suffering saint.
- God's concern and involvement is direct and intimate. He is managing every detail.
- In the end, God will bestow a far greater blessing than the suffering endured. Everything that was lost will be restored in even greater abundance.
- That permission must be granted before anything can happen to God's people.
- God is aware of our conflicts, and fully present in them. He is concerned about them, not detached from them.
- God is bigger than any circumstance and will prevail over every harmful and tragic event in life.
- We may not always understand God, but we can always believe God.
- When a saint is allowed to suffer, it is because God trusts that saint with the assignment.
- Suffering is only for a season.
- God is not the reason for the suffering, but he will use the suffering.
- The devil suffers a defeat every time a saint suffers in faith, love, and devotion to God.
- The end of our suffering is hope realized and faith actualized.

- When we choose to persevere in faith through our suffering, our outward testimony brings more glory to God than the revealed visible manifestation of His glorious created universe.

Second, we must be willing to <u>assess</u> our trials.

"My brethren, count it all joy when you fall into divers temptations; knowing this, that the trying of your faith worketh patience. But let patience have her perfect work, that ye may be perfect and entire, wanting nothing." **(James 1:2-4)** The little word ***"count"*** in this passage of Scripture speaks of a judge in the courtroom on his bench. As he tries the case before him, he has the disclosure of all the facts and evidence in front of him. Therefore, with great deliberation and discretion, he can rightly decide and make a proper judgment based on the information. By faith, when we count it all joy in our trials, the byproduct will be a deep-down, abiding assurance, creating in us a supernatural joy that transcends our natural emotions, which only produce fear. When we assess our trials, we will be brought into a realm of understanding that will cause us to see:

- A series of miraculous occurrences as the events of our trials unfold.
- An awareness of God that could never have been experienced without the trials.
- The blessings of the process as we take this journey with God.
- More clearly that this world is not our home.
- A deep sense of the mind of Christ.
- Suffering as God's chosen, anointed path by which the glories and secrets of His Personhood is revealed.
- That our future duties and responsibilities in the kingdom of God are dependent upon our suffering with Him in the present **(2 Timothy 2:11-12)**.
- That our trials complete us in Christ.

157

Third, we must give to God our utmost <u>allegiance</u> in times of severe trial.

The psalmist David emphatically stated, "In thee, O LORD, do I put my trust; let me never be ashamed: deliver me in thy righteousness. Let me not be ashamed, O LORD; for I have called upon thee: let the wicked be ashamed, and let them be silent in the grave." **(Psalms 31:1, 17)** When the journey is over, the suffering saint will never be ashamed or regret that he or she trusted completely in God. Because of what we believe about the Bible, God, heaven, eternal rewards and the grace and goodness of our Lord, all of the work and toil of our perseverance and faith will never turn out to be something that we did in vain **(1 Corinthians 15:58)**. The unbeliever who mocks, scoffs, and expresses disdain at the eternal purposes and plan of God will one day be ashamed in the presence of the Lord. These unbelievers who deny, reject, and even blaspheme the ways of our God, which they can not understand, refuse to approach and believe Him by faith. King David referred to them as "the wicked."

In the same way, when Jesus sent word back to John the Baptist answering his question, "Art thou he that should come, or do we look for another?" **(Matthew 11:3)** Jesus said, I want you to tell John "The blind receive their sight, the lame walk, the lepers are cleansed, and the deaf hear, the dead are raised up, and the poor have the gospel preached to them. And blessed is he, whosoever shall not be offended in me." **(Matthew 11:5-6)** The answer of our Lord to John the Baptist was that of reassurance.

Furthermore, the Lord, in a very loving and compassionate way, was conveying to John that everything he believed, lived, preached and taught was absolute truth. *"You will never be ashamed, John, for believing, and following me. So continue to persevere, and don't give up. I see you and know where you are. I am with you. Continue to be courageous, for you will never be ashamed that you believed!"* Unbelievers will perpetually be silent in the grave, but believers will forevermore proclaim the praises of God for His faithfulness.

Another way to show your allegiance in time of suffering is to not give up, even if you have had a failure in life. There are three reasons why we suffer:

1. Something has been taken from us.
2. Something has been done to us.
3. We have done something to ourselves (our own choosing).

Whether we have suffered because of something we have done, or because of something which was done to us, we are admonished in the Scripture to endure, persevere, and take it patiently. In God's Word there are two amazing verses coupled together that when truly understood, will bring emotional healing to a broken and damaged heart.

"For what glory is it, if, when ye be buffeted for your faults, ye shall take it patiently? But if, when ye do well, and suffer for it, ye shall take it patiently, this is acceptable with God.

For even hereunto were ye called: because Christ also suffered for us, leaving us an example, that ye should follow his steps."

(1 PETER 2:20-21)

These two verses teach us something beautiful about suffering, especially when our suffering is a result of our poor choices and failures. Both groups, those who suffer for righteous and unrighteous endeavors, can be unified in a fellowship of suffering with Him. The latter group of sufferers, as found in **1 Peter 2:20**, enter into the fellowship of Christ by taking "it patiently," persevering, and entering into the divine appointment by faith, then assessing and believing that God will accomplish a glorious outcome for the trial.

The former group can also enter into the fellowship of His suffering through the portal of confession, repentance, a humbling of oneself to God, understanding the consequence will now become a tutor and guide. This will lead the forgiven, restored, and reconciled saint into a fuller conformity of the image and likeness of Christ. This, also, is accomplished through the understanding that the reaping and consequence of wrong choices has its place in the divine appointment, assessment, and accomplishment of His purposes in our life. So praise Him! Praise Him! Praise Him! Both groups can "follow His steps" **(1 Peter 2:22)** and as a result, be in the complete will of God.

Fourth, there is a glorious <u>accomplishment</u> which God will cause to come to pass, because we acknowledged God through all of our suffering. Please read **Jeremiah 29:11 and Proverbs 3:5-7.**

The first volume of this book comes to a conclusion with the following compelling story:

When I was twenty-five years old I began my first pastorate in Rochester Hills, Michigan. There was a sweet, dear, elderly woman in our church by the name of Dixie Douglas. Dixie was a faithful saint of God. Every time the church doors were open she was there. Every special service, potluck dinner, soul winning and outreach visitation, she was present and participated. She was from the Deep South and the thing I remember most about her was her infectious laugh and her incredible dessert — Mississippi Mud Pie.

Over time, Sister Dixie became very ill. She was stricken with severe arthritis. She could no longer do for her Lord what she had done in the past. This illness hit her fast and the deterioration was very quick. Every week, sometimes a couple times each week, I would go to Dixie's house to encourage her with prayer, the Word of God, and with the presence of her pastor, whom she loved very much.

I recall the many times I sat there with Dixie, watching her weep profusely and crying with anguish. The question was always the same, "O Pastor, why am I suffering so much? Why can't I do the things for God I used to do? Why is our Lord allowing these things to happen to me? I just don't understand..."

As a young, inexperienced pastor, I didn't know what to say. All I could do was rely on my training, and that wasn't good enough for this situation. I would go home after visiting with Dixie and plead with God, "O Lord, please show me something. Give me something I can share with Dixie to help her feel better." I would repeat this ritual week after week, but then, all of the sudden, God gave to me the incredible truth which forever changed my life and helped that dear, precious, saint of God. I'll never forget that night. I ran out of my home, jumped in the car, and with great alacrity drove to Dixie's house. It was dark out and somewhat late, but it didn't matter. I had to get this truth personally to Dixie. It is found in the following passage:

"Wherein ye greatly rejoice, though now for a season, if need be, ye are in heaviness through manifold temptations: that the trial of your faith, being much more precious than of gold that perisheth, though it be tried with fire, might be found unto praise and honour and glory at the appearing of Jesus Christ: Whom having not seen, ye love; in whom, though now ye see him not, yet believing, ye rejoice with joy unspeakable and full of glory: Receiving the end of your faith, even the salvation of your souls."

(1 PETER 1:6-9)

Upon arriving at Dixie's house, I ran to her door and began to pound aggressively. Through the door, I could hear her feeble voice saying,

"Who is it?" I replied with much excitement, "It's me Dixie! Pastor! Let me in, please! I have something important to share with you!"

Upon opening the door, with her deep, unique, southern drawl she exclaimed, "Pastor! Pastor! What's going on?"

I said, "Dixie, I have a truth from God I must share with you right now. Please sit down." After reading **1 Peter 1:6-9**, I went on to explain, "Dixie, according to this passage, you can offer to God all of your sickness, hurt, pain, sorrow, suffering, doubt, fear and anguish. You can place all of these afflictions on the altar of sacrifice and offer them to Him as a sweet smelling savor in the nostrils of God. As you do this in faith, you will be saying to God, 'In all of my sufferings, I will still love, honor, serve, adore, and worship you.' Dixie, upon our Lord's return, every day, hour, and minute of your suffering will shine as gold before every person. The multitudes of humanity, past, present, and future, on earth, in heaven, and under the earth, the entire universe of beings, celestial and terrestrial, will bring praise, honor, glory, worship, and thanksgiving to Him *"at the appearing of Jesus Christ."* Why? Because they saw in you, Dixie, this wonderful, suffering saint, who made such a sacrifice of a love offering to her Lord!"

Dixie, without hesitation, accepted this truth. She saw and understood it as a personal message from the Lord to her. The moment she heard these words, I saw the supernatural peace and comfort of God give to her a beautiful, heavenly rest.

Suffering saint, consider the magnitude and the endless scope of glory you can bring to your Lord when you suffer in such a manner as described in this book. You will allow an infinity of blessings to be bestowed on you and others, not only in this life, but also in that which is to come. Be blessed and know in your moments of severe suffering, **you will able to see some things, hear some things, experience some things, know some things, and understand some things that otherwise you would've never been able to see, hear, experience, know or understand had God not allowed you to go through this time of suffering.**

Bibliography

Carroll, J.M. *The Trail of Blood.* Lexington, Ky.: Ashland Avenue
Baptist Church, 1931.

Dobson, J.C. *When God Doesn't Make Sense.* Carol Stream, Ill.: Tyndale
House Publishers, 1997.

Earley, D. *21 Reasons Bad Things Happen to Good People.* Uhrichsville,
Ohio: Barbour Publishing, Inc., 2007.

Jennings, F. *Dake's Annotated Reference Bible.* Lawrenceville, Ga.: Dake
Bible, Inc., 1963.

Knight, W.B. *Knight's Master Book of 4,000 Illustrations.* Grand Rapids:
William B. Eerdmans Publishing, 1956.

Lahaye, T. *Revelation Unveiled.* Grand Rapids: Zondervan, 1999.

Seamonds, D. *Healing for Damaged Emotions.* Wheaton: Victor Books,
1981.

Strong, J. *Strong's Exhaustive Concordance of the Bible.* Iowa Falls:
Riverside Book and Bible House, 1890.

Thomas, Edwin. "How Do Farmers Sift Wheat?" Career Trend, 25
July 2017, careertrend.com/how-does-4925686-farmers-sift-
wheat.html.

Torrey, R.A. *The New Topical Textbook.* Murfreesboro, Tenn.: Sword of
the Lord Publishers, 1897.

Willmington, H.L. *Willmington's Guide to the Bible.* Wheaton: Tyndale
House, 1981.

ACKNOWLEDGMENTS

S pecial thanks to my beautiful niece Rebecca (4.0) Schweitzer, who spent countless hours proofreading and editing with me.

Special thanks to Lynne Tagawa, who did all the initial proofreading and editing.

Special thanks to JB, John Bologna, our ministry business manager, for his faithfulness, benevolence, encouragement and vision.

About the Author

D r. T. A. "Shrek" Nalian, the founder of the Stand Strength Team and of the Hymns Project music group, has been a motivational speaker and evangelist for over 28 years. He has conducted countless public school assemblies and has been a guest speaker for many colleges, universities, businesses, churches, special interest groups, and prisons. Multitudes of lives have been impacted and changed by his message!

He believes that every person has more ability, potential, and talent than they will use in a lifetime. As a child, he was greatly abused at home and bullied at school. He understands that perseverance and hard work and a close walk with Christ can overcome insurmountable odds and suffering. Dr. Nalian's vision is to not only reach the youth and families our nation with the Gospel of Jesus Christ. He also recognizes the complex challenges people face. With this book, his hope and prayer are that readers would know true comfort, healing, deliverance and hope.

Synopsis

G od wants to show you, in your time of suffering, that you can see some things, know some things, understand some things that otherwise you would have never experienced without the journey of suffering.

In this book, Dr. T.A. Nalian offers an in-depth study of the Biblical formula to understanding our suffering from the origin of our suffering to realizing the hope, comfort, contentment and victory Christ Jesus has already given us in our times of suffering.